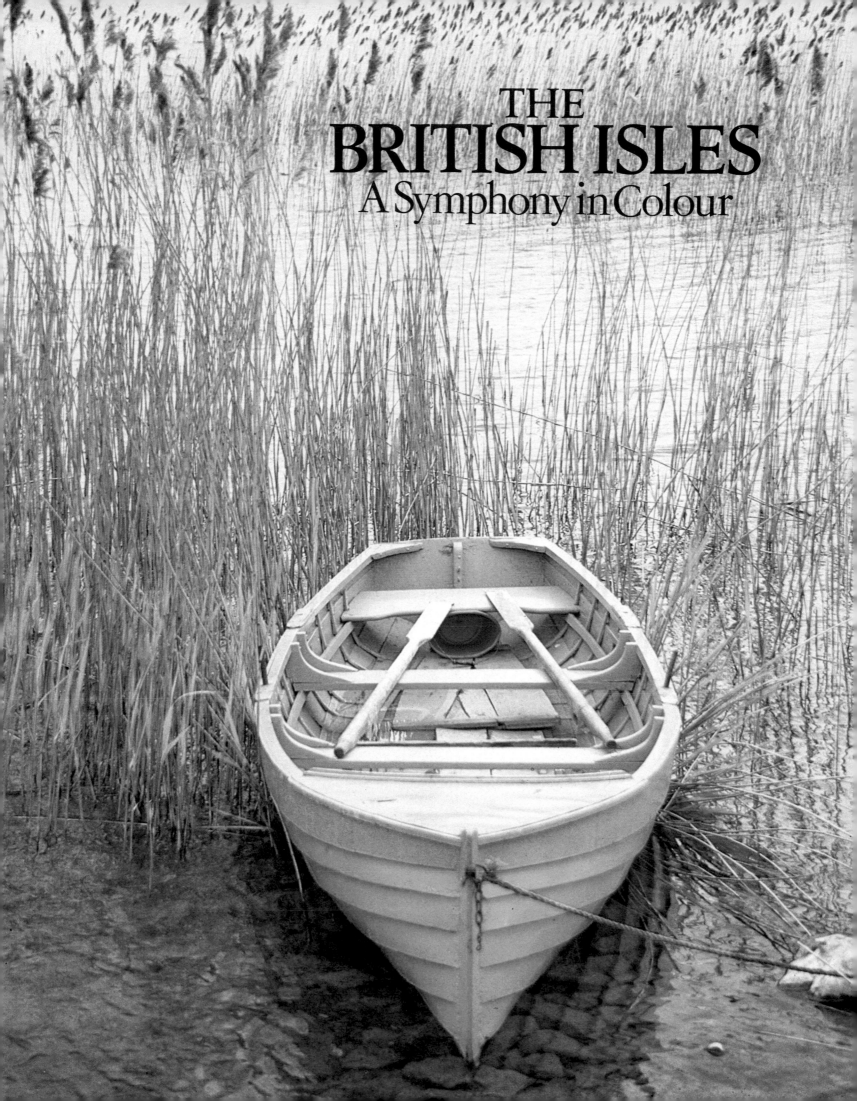

THE
BRITISH ISLES
A Symphony in Colour

Producer:	Ted Smart.
Editor:	David Gibbon.
Designer:	Philip Clucas.
Staff Writers:	Lee Thomas
	Kathryn Spink.
Researcher:	Hanni Edmonds.

First published in Great Britain 1980 by
Colour Library International Ltd.
© 1980 Illustrations and text:
Colour Library International Ltd.,
New Malden, Surrey, England.
Colour separations by
FERCROM, Barcelona, Spain.
Display and text filmsetting by
Focus Photoset, London, England.
Printed and bound by
JISA-RIEUSSET, Barcelona, Spain.
ISBN 0 906558-50-6
COLOUR LIBRARY INTERNATIONAL

THE
BRITISH ISLES
A Symphony in Colour

COLOUR LIBRARY INTERNATIONAL

THE BRITISH ISLES
'A SYMPHONY IN COLOUR'

CONTENTS

7
FOREWORD
by the Marquess of Bath

10–41
LONDON
by David Gibbon

42–51
ROYAL FAMILY
by Don Coolican

52–163
ENGLAND
by Lee Thomas

164–227
CATHEDRALS
by Philip Clucas

228–235
CRAFTS
by David Gibbon

236–249
WALES
by David Gibbon

250–309
SCOTLAND
by Ian Digby

310–375
IRELAND
by Terence J. Sheehy

376–383
MAPS

Foreword

'There are no countries in the world less known by the British than these self same British Islands.'

George Borrow (1803-1881) Preface to Lavengro.

I do not necessarily agree wholeheartedly with the sentiments of the rather cynical 19th century writer, nevertheless there is still an element of truth, even a century later, in what he wrote.

It has become far too fashionable 'to be going abroad for one's holiday'. Indeed, it is quite remarkable that it is almost assumed that holiday plans *necessitate* travel away from our shores – the result, no doubt, of the excellent marketing of cheap air flights and overseas accommodation.

However, nowhere in the world can any countries of comparable size boast of so much to be seen as there is here – in Britain. We have it all, and, what is more, one never has to travel very far – these 'tight little isles' are conveniently compact.

What a blessing that the preservationists and conservationists have managed so successfully to eliminate hoardings from the roadsides, and to retain so much of our countryside and shoreline as totally unspoilt areas. There are many country lanes barely the width of one's car waiting to be explored, winding through charming villages and hamlets which have remained unchanged since time immemorial.

Our cities, culture and countryside cannot be excelled in my view – browse through this book and you will be left in no doubt that I am right by the time you reach its end.

Bath

LONGLEAT HOUSE
WARMINSTER, WILTS.

. . . The peace and wildness of offshore islands; the grandeur of the Highlands; soft Welsh valleys, Satanic mills; emerald green pastures; windswept moors; gentle downlands and a people fashioned by their rich, rich history – of such are these islands – the British Isles.

Near Simonsbath the River Barle winds snake-like across Exmoor below and not far from Broadway the rich countryside of Worcestershire right rolls gently away into the distant hills.

LONDON

'When a man is tired of London,
he is tired of life,
for there is in London
all that life can afford.'

These famous words of Dr Johnson are as true today as when he uttered them 200 years ago. London can claim as much, if not more, variety of atmosphere, culture, entertainment, tradition and architecture as any city on earth: it is, as William Dunbar was to claim, 'the flower of cities all'.

Packed into the 610 square miles of Greater London – Europe's largest city – are a wealth of concert halls, art galleries, museums, parks and gardens, theatres, cinemas, restaurants and famous buildings which in recent years have drawn increasing numbers of tourists from Europe, the Far East and particularly the United States. More than ten million people now visit Britain each year and nearly all of them will spend part of their holiday in the capital.

With its 'bobbies', its red double-decker buses and its famous underground system among its most instantly identifiable features, London has an unhurried air of permanence reinforced by the durability of its great institutions such as the Tower, St

Night-time highlights the familiar landmarks of England's majestic capital, among them the imposing Clock Tower of Big Ben, which rises as a symbol of London above the evening traffic in Whitehall left. Equally well-known Piccadilly Circus above parades the vivid display of neon signs for which it has become famous.

Familiar red London buses cross Lambeth Bridge, above right against the background of the city's old skyline while the Post Office Tower top presents a more futuristic profile. This soaring tribute to modern design houses, in addition to a great deal of technological hardware, a revolving restaurant.

LONDON

Pauls, Buckingham Palace and Big Ben.

There is much more to London than visits to these famous tourist spots. The traveller who forsakes the guided tours for a day or two and wanders at will will come across some of the winding streets and narrow alleys so reminiscent of the city Dickens knew. One of the pleasures of London is that so much can be seen on foot – safely and without needing to walk more than two or three miles a day.

Starting perhaps from Piccadilly Circus – once regarded as the hub of the old British Empire – head south down Lower Regent Street into St James's, which has remained largely unchanged for three centuries. Continue down St James's Street to St James's Palace, built by Henry VIII as a royal residence, until Queen Victoria forsook it for Buckingham Palace at the start of her reign. But its links with the British Royal Family remain, albeit tenuously. When a new foreign ambassador arrives to take up residence in London he establishes his right to do so by presenting his credentials 'at the Court of St James'.

St James's also houses two of London's leading clubs for gentlemen – the Reform in Pall Mall where Jules Verne's Phileas Fogg set off to travel Around the World in Eighty Days, and the distinguished Athenaeum whose members include many Lords, knights, government ministers and leading figures of the arts, sciences and public life. Close by, in St James's Street itself, are two delightful old shops which have been catering to the needs of such club members for more than a century: Lobbs, whose tailor-made shoes adorn the feet of royalty and the famous, and Lock's who have been making hats for more than two hundred years.

A ten-minute walk across St James's Park leads into Whitehall where the solid facades of government buildings look on to quiet quadrangles and

An infinite variety of moods makes up the life of London: Piccadilly Circus right has its occasional deserted moments and in the quiet of the night Chelsea Bridge above far right shimmers on undisturbed waters. A traditional 'pub' far right provides a more congested retreat. Some of the veterans of the Chelsea Royal Hospital proudly display their medals above right and overleaf a military parade passes with vivid pomp.

LONDON

discreet side streets. Even Downing Street, where the Prime Minister resides at Number Ten, has an air on an early Sunday morning of a respectable little residential street. Only the ever-present policeman at the door suggests something more significant.

Up Whitehall, into Trafalgar Square to feed the perpetually hungry pigeons and to admire the 200-foot-high Nelson's Column and Landseer's Lions, then up into St Martin's Lane where every other building seems to be a pub or a theatre. On both sides of this attractive street are a host of little

courts and alleys, well stocked with specialist and antiquarian bookshops and antique dealers. In Goodwin's Court, off to the right, there are some delightful Georgian houses now occupied exclusively by people or companies connected with the arts – writers, publishers, film companies and so on.

Continue up St Martin's Lane, through Cambridge Circus and into Charing Cross Road, the centre of London's book trade, then turn left into the narrow streets of world-famous Soho.

Soho was developed after the Great Fire of London, but little of it now dates back more than a hundred years or so. It lies on the site of old hunting grounds. 'So ho!' was the shout that used to go up when the hunter spotted a quarry. Soho's chief appeal these days is not its reputation for naughty night-clubs – most are nothing more than tawdry – but its cheerful cosmopolitan character. Excellent continental restaurants, German and Scandinavian delicatessens, Italian bakers and French patisseries make it a delight for the gourmet.

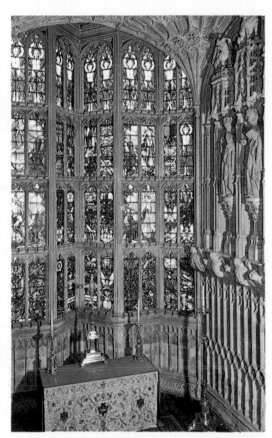

The lakes and fountains of Trafalgar Square above left provide a welcome oasis for the weary sightseer. The origins of the Tower of London left date back to William the Conqueror. Its solid and uncompromising walls attract visitors for many reasons: its historic associations, the Crown Jewels housed within and the spectacle of the Yeoman Warders above as they go about their duties in their colourful costumes. Tower Bridge top provides yet another impressive sight, and the lovely stained-glass window above right in the Royal Air Force Memorial Chapel in Westminster Abbey commemorates the airmen who lost their lives in the Battle of Britain.

Shaftesbury Avenue, at the southern end of Soho, leads back into Piccadilly Circus. Going west from there, along Piccadilly itself, there is much to see. On the left, almost immediately is a Wren Church, St James's, with some superb wood carvings by Grinling Gibbons, whose work graces many fine old houses and stately homes in southern England. Further along is Hatchards, one of London's leading booksellers; and Fortnum and Mason, the food emporium with delicacies from all over the world, is always worth a visit, though the shopper on a limited budget should proceed with caution. Linger, too, to watch the wall clock outside Fortnum's with its beautiful little figures that make an appearance every

LONDON

hour and half hour with the clock's chimes.

On to the other – the north – side of Piccadilly and look for Albany standing back in its own quiet little courtyard away from the hustle and bustle of Piccadilly. It is a distinguished old house built at the end of the eighteenth century and now divided into exclusive apartments. One recent distinguished resident was Edward Heath, the former Prime Minister. Further along is Burlington House, where the Royal Academy of Art stages major exhibitions, and Burlington Arcade, reputed to be the world's longest and oldest (opened in 1819) covered walk, lined by the most attractive little shops selling jewellery, militaria, perfume and examples of British craftsmanship such as woven tartan.

Down past Green Park tube station and Green Park itself laps up to the railings of Piccadilly on the South side. Here on Sunday mornings, amateur painters from the talented to the merely enthusiastic, hang their latest masterpieces available for sale for as little as £5.

Before reaching Hyde Park Corner at the end of Piccadilly, dive down the narrow White Horse Street to the right and wander round a genuine London village – Shepherd Market, with its own distinct character formed by pavement cafés, several excellent restaurants, two or three extremely sociable pubs and some quaint little shops where personal service is the criterion of the proprietor.

Shepherd Market lies at the south end of Mayfair. Several elegant streets lead north into Grosvenor Square over which the massive eagle of the impressive American Embassy keeps beady-eyed watch. Continue north into Oxford Street but delay the shopping expedition there until you have walked up towards Marble Arch, where the Arch itself is sited close to the spot where the Tyburn Gallows dispatched many a villain in days gone by. For 600 years, until 1783, Londoners gathered here to watch public executions, a favourite form of entertainment. Cross over to the corner of Hyde Park where, if it's Sunday afternoon, you'll experience one of the great free entertainments London can offer – Speaker's Corner. Here, anyone can stand on his own soapbox, and speak publicly on any subject he likes. He or

Right: *Admiralty Arch.*

she will be assured of a big audience and a lot of good natured heckling. The Corner has its own 'regular' speakers who are quite accomplished, and occasionally public figures will also come to speak, subject to the same heckling as any other. But they enter the spirit of the location, giving no quarter and expecting none.

Walk back along Oxford Street, allowing plenty of time to sample the wares of what is probably the city's major shopping street. Among the tried and tested attractions are general stores like Selfridges, Marks & Spencer, John Lewis, Marshall & Snelgrove, and, for music enthusiasts, the HMV record shop that caters for every music taste from classical to jazz, rock and punk. Continue along to Oxford Circus, then turn right into one of London's most classically elegant streets – Regent Street. It was originally designed by the architect John Nash to provide the Prince Regent, later George IV, with a direct route between his palace and Regent's Park, but little of the original conception remains. However, the curving sweep of the street is still impressive and some of the shops – Liberty and Dickins and Jones among them – are London's most sophisticated.

Holborn and Bloomsbury, lying about a mile to the east of Piccadilly Circus, are well worth a visit. Here the presence of business offices is more obvious than further west but this does not detract from the area. It gives W.C.1. (west central postal region) a character of its own. It contains many places of interest – the Inns of Court, the British Museum, the University of London and numerous pleasant walks through courtyards and narrow streets. The name Holborn is thought to derive from the old English word 'Bourne' meaning river or stream. The original area was a low-lying tract of ground, a hole, near the old Fleet River

London has a wealth of fine theatres offering first-class entertainment, among them the original home of the hit musical 'Jesus Christ – Superstar' above left, Wyndhams left, the Ambassador top right, the Windmill centre right, the Aldwych right and the National Theatre below far right. The Royal Ballet above far right is one of London's two principal ballet companies.

The Clock Tower of Big Ben soars above the Palace of Westminster overleaf.

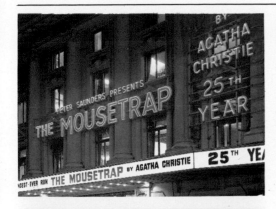

LONDON

which now runs underground north of Fleet Street. Just to the south of Holborn (the street) lies Lincoln's Inn, one of London's four Inns of Court, the others being Gray's Inn, and the Inner and Middle Temples. Here a lawyer learns his profession, usually as a member of chambers – a firm to whom he is articled or apprenticed. Law has been practised on the site of Lincoln's Inn since the thirteenth century; although nothing remains from that time, much of the existing architecture is Tudor. Like the other Inns, Lincoln's Inn has an air of unhurried calm and tranquillity about it. Benches are dotted about the little courtyards and paths for those requiring a period of quiet contemplation. The Inner and Middle Temples, just the other side of Fleet Street, were called by Charles Lamb *the most elegant spot in the metropolis* with their beautifully kept lawns and gardens. These inns were originally owned by the Crusading

London's parks, gardens and open spaces provide idyllic retreats from the city's congestion. A military band performs in St James's Park above right, schoolgirls gather off Sloane Street above and pleasure barges carry visitors through 'Little Venice' left while, on the Regent's Park Canal right, a narrow boat makes its way towards Camden Lock.

LONDON

Knights Templar, hence the name, and there are still strong connections and traditions dating back to the time of the Crusades. Adjoining Lincoln's Inn are Lincoln's Inn Fields, a large open square, with tennis courts and expanses of grass, occupied during summer weekdays by office workers with their sandwiches, but at weekends a quiet oasis in the heart of the city.

Further down Holborn towards Holborn Circus, a turning to the left leads into Hatton Garden, where diamond merchants, some in what now look like rundown premises, carry on their lucrative trade. And further along Holborn, across the viaduct that takes the road over what was the Fleet valley, lies the Old Bailey, housing the Central Criminal Courts, where many of the most famous cases in the history of British justice have taken place. Earlier on this site stood the infamous Newgate Prison where public hangings were a frequent occurrence.

Retracing the way back along Holborn and then turning north at Southampton Row, Bloomsbury lies to the left. Bloomsbury is the literary centre of London where many publishers still have their offices. Much of the architecture is Georgian and the area is pinpointed with attractive squares and the two major sites of the

London is far more than a collection of historic buildings, grand hotels, such as Claridge's left, or renowned establishments like Sotheby's above. It is also a thriving community of people, such as the flower vendor right, whose blooms bring colour to the city streets.

28

British Museum and the University of London. Literary connections and associations are visible in almost every street with blue wall plaques indicating the reason. Disraeli lived in Bloomsbury as a young man and the so-called Bloomsbury Set, ruled by Virginia Woolf, held court there in the 1920s.

Dante Gabriel Rossetti lived in Red Lion Square (claimed to be a haunt of Cromwell's spectre) and a short distance away in Doughty Street Charles Dickens kept house for three years. It is now maintained as a museum and library open to the public.

To the south of Holborn lie the Strand (meaning 'beach' which once it was to the Thames) and, where the City of London begins at Temple Bar, Fleet Street, the centre of the newspaper industry. Three major London theatres line the Strand, as well as some interesting shops, but a diversion to the north leads to Covent Garden, once the site of the famous vegetable market, now transported across the river to the Nine Elms site. Still in Covent Garden is the Inigo Jones church of St Paul's, set in the centre of a square which Shaw used for the opening scene in *Pygmalion,* later staged and filmed as *My Fair Lady.* Nearby is the Royal Opera House and the Theatre Royal, Drury Lane where *My Fair Lady* opened in London. A theatre has been on this site since 1663 but the present one dates from the early 1800s.

Between the Strand and the Thames is a pub called the Gilbert and Sullivan in John Adam Street (the area was built by the Adam brothers but little remains of their designs now). The pub has charming models of the operas dotted around its walls and mementos of W.S. Gilbert and Arthur Sullivan; very appropriate, because only a few hundred yards away, next to the famous hotel of the same name, is the Savoy Theatre where many of the original Gilbert and Sullivan operettas were first performed.

Towards the end of the Strand, and just before the Central Law Courts, is the Aldwych, at which theatre the

Among the many masterpieces housed in London's National Gallery are Anthony van Dyck's 'Equestrian Portrait of Charles I' left, Thomas Gainsborough's 'Mr and Mrs Andrews' above right and Rembrandt's 'Hendrickje Stoffels' right.

LONDON

Royal Shakespeare Company has its London headquarters. And just beyond there is the church of St Clement Danes, built by Wren, which has been immortalised in the famous nursery rhyme, *'Oranges and Lemons, say the bells of St Clements.'* Dr Johnson was a regular worshipper at the church, living a five-minute walk away in Gough Square – a turning to the left off Fleet Street leads to it. His house at no. 17 remains a fine example of Queen Anne architecture. Fleet Street itself now houses only two national newspapers, The Daily Telegraph and the Daily Express, but most of the others, as well as many provincial newspapers, have offices in the neighbourhood.

The continuation of Fleet Street – Ludgate Hill – leads up past St Pauls and into the City of London proper. The 'square mile', as it is known, stretches along the north bank of the Thames from Temple Bar to the Tower of London. It is governed by the Lord Mayor and his Court of Aldermen and even the Queen, traditionally, has to seek the Mayor's permission before entering. The City has its own police force and courts of law and during the working day upwards of half a million people earn their living there in the commercial heart of the capital. But by the weekend the City is populated by just 5,000 residents. Its street names indicate the trades and markets that used to flourish there – Bread Street (where John Milton was born), Wood Street, Ironmonger Lane and Poultry.

Near Bread Street, which runs into Cheapside, is the church of St Mary-le-Bow. To have been born within the sound of its bells – Bow Bells – is necessary for anyone who calls himself a cockney. And it was these same bells that summoned Dick Whittington back to become three times Lord Mayor of London, according to the legend.

Among the institutions in the City are the Mansion House, (the Lord Mayor's official residence), the Bank of England, the Monument designed by Wren to commemorate the Great Fire of London, the Royal Exchange (no longer in commercial use but once the market place for traders in agricultural produce), and the Guildhall where the Lord Mayor and his Sheriffs are elected. The first Guildhall was built in the early fifteenth century, but much of what can be seen now dates from the seventeenth century. Look for

the memorials to two great Englishmen, Lord Nelson and Sir Winston Churchill, and the statues of two great figures of legend, Gog and Magog.

Just over the River lies the South Bank, redeveloped since World War Two and providing Londoners and visitors alike with a wealth of cultural

Also in the National Gallery are 'Susanna Lunden' ('Le Chapeau de Paille') above, the work of Peeter Pauwel Rubens, and the magnificent 'Wilton Diptych', a detail of which is shown above right.

possibilities. Nestling against Waterloo Bridge is the New National Theatre and within a few hundred yards are the National Film Theatre, the Hayward Gallery, which has a deserved reputation for presenting the best of new developments in art, and the Queen Elizabeth Hall, a concert hall specialising in chamber and ensemble music. Further along is the Royal Festival Hall, built to commemorate the 1951 Festival of Britain and now probably London's leading concert hall for orchestral and ballet works. Further on is the impressive County Hall, headquarters for the giant Greater London Council, the administrative body for the whole of London, apart from the City. Continuing the riverside walk, one comes to St Mary's Church tucked close beside the grandeur of Lambeth Palace. Here Captain Bligh – Bligh of the Bounty – lies buried.

Lambeth Palace is the official

Other superb paintings in this collection include Raphael's 'St Catherine of Alexandria' left; Renoir's 'The Umbrellas' above, and 'A Boy Aged Eleven' by Jacob van Oost I top.

residence of the Archbishops of Canterbury. The site dates back to the thirteenth century and landmarks of English ecclesiastical history are set there: the English prayer book was composed at Lambeth by Cranmer,

LONDON

conflicts of Church and State have taken place there and the evolution of the English Protestant Church has been planned and supervised there for centuries. It is not open to the public, except by appointment, but it is well worth a visit to ponder such affairs from the outside.

The walk along the South Bank, particularly when the Thames is in full spate, is a memorable experience. The skyline on the opposite, northern bank, with such profiles as St Pauls, Big Ben and the House of Commons clearly visible is truly impressive. A summer's evening there with London's lights beginning to flicker on is an ideal conclusion to a first visit to the city that Heinrich Heine once described as *'the greatest wonder which the world can show to the astonished spirit'.*

Historic London

London evolved as two entirely separate towns – the walled fortress founded by the Romans about AD 43

and the settlement that grew around the site of Westminster Abbey some 900 years later, the two separated by no more than a mile or two of marshy ground.

The Roman town developed after they forded the Thames between the gravel banks of what is now Ludgate Hill on the north bank and Southwark on the south, to allow their troops and transport, landing on the Kentish coast, access to their chief city, Colchester, to the north east and their further flung outposts to the north and west. Within a few years this crossing point became the hub of Roman activities in Britain, with Watling Street serving it from the south, running on north along the line of what is now the Edgware Road to St Albans and eventually to the border country

Her Majesty the Queen returns the salute during the 'Trooping of the Colour' left and right.

Nightfall brings a special magic to Trafalgar Square below.

LONDON

where Hadrian left his famous mark on the landscape: and other roads leading from it to feed Chichester, Silchester, Lincoln and York.

Under the Emperor Constantius, whose wife was a Briton, London flourished and at the beginning of the 3rd century AD its citizens enjoyed a standard of living that, according to historians, was not attained again until nearly 1,500 years later. But it was shortlived, as was the Roman presence in Britain, and with the legions' departure the country under the Angles, Saxons and Jutes reverted to a farming economy – London was largely abandoned.

The Norman William was good for London: he rebuilt its fortifications, added the castle (now the part of the Tower known as the White Tower), had

A statue of Sir Winston Churchill left serves as a reminder of past greatness while below, is shown St Paul's Cathedral, the imposing masterpiece of Sir Christopher Wren.

LONDON

another church built on the St Pauls site (later to be destroyed by fire) and perhaps most importantly, granted a charter to the merchants of the city which laid down a measure of independence for it that the City still enjoys today in certain respects. The merchants were not slow to exercise this independence when they met at St Pauls to appoint Prince John Regent to Richard I in place of Richard's own choice whom they disliked. But John had to pay a price: in 1192 he established the city as a municipal corporation with its own mayor, later to be dignified as the Lord Mayor – an extremely influential position. Even today it is laid down that the Lord Mayor is among the first to be officially informed of a monarch's death and is traditionally the first to be summoned to a meeting of the Privy Council that announces the monarch's successor. Just twenty years later, the City had had enough of John and forced him to grant the Magna Carta which said specifically of the capital: 'Let the City of London have all its liberties and its free customs, as well by land as by water.'

Business continued to dominate

Darkness softens the familiar outlines of London's historic buildings: left the Houses of Parliament with Lambeth Bridge in the foreground, centre left Buckingham Palace, top left the dome of St Paul's Cathedral rising above Fleet Street, and above Big Ben seen across the River Thames.

London life and not even the Black Death, from which 50,000 died and were alleged to have been buried in the 'smooth-field' (the site of Smithfield), seriously halted progress. The Guildhall was completed in 1425 and by Tudor times Smithfield and Cheapside were two of Europe's chief markets where, for instance, German clocks, French wines and Venetian glassware were sold alongside British cloth.

With the arrival of Henry VIII on the throne, Westminster's destiny was uprooted. He moved the court out of Westminster Palace in favour of the Palace of Whitehall, formerly the London residence of the Archbishops of York. And with the dissolution of the monasteries Westminster Abbey became a protestant church and St Stephen's Hall the home of the Commons.

By the time the first Elizabeth was

Ceremonies such as the Changing of the Guard at Buckingham Palace, Mounting the Guard at Horse Guards Parade, Gun Salutes to mark important anniversaries and the Trooping of the Colour on the Queen's official birthday, bring breathtaking colour to the life of England's capital.

LONDON

on the throne the combined population of London and Westminster was around 300,000, living largely in cramped, dirty accommodation, made no better by sewage that constantly ran down the streets from the overflowing Fleet River. This, and the continual demolition and rebuilding of these times, led to a steady stream of removals from the City to Westminster and the land between, but it was a war – the Civil War of Roundheads and Cavaliers – that finally brought the unification of London and Westminster into the largest city in Europe. Earthworks were built as defence against the Royalist troops, stretching from the Tower in the east, running parallel between the Fleet and the Thames, and around the Palace of Westminster.

Twenty years later the old London disappeared, first in the Plague which accounted for more than 50,000 lives,

then in the Great Fire of 1666 which burned for four days, demolished 13,000 dwellings and left 200,000 homeless, many of them camped in the open outside the city walls. However, it gave the city fathers an opportunity which Sir Christopher Wren grasped for the redesigning of London and although his first imaginative plan was

St Katherine's Yacht Haven above right provides relatively peaceful moorings. Featured right are the impressive Law Courts of Temple Bar while the crowned and blindfolded figure of Justice above stands atop the most famous of all the London courts, the Old Bailey.

LONDON

turned down on the grounds of cost, a new London started to emerge, part of which was St Pauls, finally completed in 1710. London now stretched into Bloomsbury, and, after King William moved the court to St James's Palace, into the area north of the Palace called Piccadilly. The Strand area between London and Westminster was elegantly developed by the Adams brothers; Soho and Regent Street were put on the map and the Fleet River was covered over and condemned to an underground existence. By the early nineteenth century the Georgian era was leaving a beauty mark on the face of London: the work of Nash adorned Regent Street and Buckingham Palace into which Victoria moved on her accession, after George III bought it from the Buckingham family.

The railway reached London in 1836 and, with its rapid development, suburbia and the commuter arrived. People were able to live outside the traditional square mile and the West End, as it came to be known, and still travel reasonably cheaply and comfortably to work.

The First World War gave London a taste of aerial warfare but it was not until 1940 that the true effects were felt when hundreds of enemy bombers and rockets filled the London sky. In those dark years, 29,000 Londoners died, 240,000 houses were destroyed and major damage was caused to such buildings as Buckingham Palace, the House of Commons and Westminster Abbey. Nearly half the city's churches were devastated. The cost of rebuilding was terrifying and it took London nearly twenty years to obliterate most of the scars – the bomb sites that once littered the city.

London Pageantry

London is rich in pageantry. At almost any time of the year it can be glimpsed by the discerning visitor, while to many Londoners it has become almost an unremarkable part of daily life, be it the Changing of the Guard in the forecourt of Buckingham Palace, the cheery Beefeater in his sumptuous uniform at the Tower, the Chelsea Pensioners occasionally to be seen taking the sun along the Chelsea Embankment, or even the old brewer's dray with its top-hatted driver perched high above the

Visitors pause in Trafalgar Square left to watch the pigeons, for which it has become renowned.

LONDON

magnificent horse-drawn relic of Edwardian days. All these, in their different ways, are part of London's heritage.

But to most people the city's pageantry means the beautiful set-pieces brilliantly stage-managed every year in a style internationally acknowledged to be second to none; such events as the Lord Mayor's Show, the State Opening of Parliament and Trooping the Colour.

The Lord Mayor's Show is held on the first Saturday after the 9th November – the day on which, each year, a new Lord Mayor is elected. A long, colourful procession of carriages and floats, at times resembling more a carnival in atmosphere, winds its way through streets lined with cheering Londoners, from the Guildhall, the City's seat of government, to the Law Courts in the Strand. It is led by the new Mayor waving to his citizens from a beautiful coach built in 1757 and drawn by six magnificent brewers' horses. He has an escort of pikemen resplendent in the old uniforms of the Honourable Artillery Company of Pikemen and Musketeers, thought to be the oldest regiment in the world still in existence. His coach is followed by

On a winter evening the Clock Tower, which houses Big Ben, glows with a welcome light left and Christmas tree lights bring a festive atmosphere to Trafalgar Square above.

The winged and gilded figure right crowns the Victoria Memorial in Queen's Gardens.

LONDON

detachments from the three armed services accompanied by military bands. Each year the procession has a theme – flowers, the river, old London and so on – which is reflected in a series of beautifully designed floats put together by City associations, companies, guilds etc. The ceremony has its origins in the agreement made seven hundred years ago with King John which guaranteed the city's independence, in return for which each year the new Mayor should travel from the City to pay his respects to the Monarch. It certainly sets London alight on what is usually a damp, drizzly November day.

The State Opening of Parliament occurs with each new session of Parliament and is opened by a speech from the monarch of the day outlining the government's forthcoming legislative plans. The speech itself is usually remarkable for its lack of controversy or drama (it is written for the sovereign by the government of the time). But the procession to the House of Lords (the monarch always addresses her Lords with the Commons in attendance) from Buckingham Palace more than makes up for this. The Queen makes the journey in the superb Irish State Coach and is escorted by the Household Cavalry on their magnificent steeds. The short route is lined by the Brigade of Guards and the procession is, each year, Londoners' major opportunity to salute their Queen. The Opening is also marked by a 41-gun Royal Salute fired in nearby St James's Park.

The Trooping the Colour: A 'colour' is the ceremonial flag of a battalion or regiment, and 'trooping' means marching to music. This splendid ceremony is held on the Sovereign's official birthday, the second Saturday in June (the Queen's actual birthday being 21 April). Dressed in the uniform of colonel of the regiment, she rides side-saddle from Buckingham Palace, down the Mall, turning right into Horseguards Parade just before Admiralty Arch. There she takes the salute as the scarlet-uniformed, bear-skinned Brigade of Guards (consisting of Grenadiers, Coldstreams, Scots, Irish and Welsh Guards), together with massed bands, put on an impressive display of precision marching. If it is a hot day it's not unusual for one or two guardsmen in their close-fitting uniforms to pass out on the parade ground, an event traditionally recorded in the following day's newspapers. But if it is wet, the ceremony is usually cancelled because of the damage the rain would do to the costly uniforms.

These are but a few of the pageants of London which bring to those who watch them an indelible sense of the tradition and history inherent in the city.

The County Hall above left, the blaze of lights which herald Piccadilly Circus left, a secluded corner of the Tower of London above, the Lord Mayor's elaborate coach above right and the illuminations of Albert Bridge right... all form part of the ever-varying tapestry that is London.

ROYAL FAMILY

Queen Elizabeth II rules by the rights of a constitution that goes back eleven centuries. The monarchy is the oldest secular institution in Britain, tracing its origins to 829; that was the year the Saxon King Egbert united England when he became King of Wessex and All England. The Queen traces her descent from Egbert, who reigned for twelve years.

According to some genealogists, the Royal Family can also claim in its ancestry the Prophet of Islam, Mohammed, and the first President of the United States, George Washington. As well as being related to almost every past and present royal family in Europe for over 150 years – thanks to the prolific breeding of Queen Victoria – The Queen and her children also include a few ordinary Smiths and Browns in their backgrounds.

Until the First World War the family belonged to the House of Saxe-Coburg and Gotha, a link with Queen Victoria's

prince consort who was Prince Albert of Saxe-Coburg and Gotha. Feelings were running so high against Germany during the war that King George V made a proclamation in 1917 that Windsor would be the family name of all Queen Victoria's male descendants and in April 1952, before her coronation, Queen Elizabeth II declared that she and all her children should be known as the House and Family of Windsor.

The monarchy is four centuries older than Parliament and three centuries older than the British judicial system. Its continuity has been broken only once – that was the eleven years from 1649 to 1660, when Britain was governed by Oliver Cromwell. Up to the end of the seventeenth century, when Parliament established a monarchy with limited rights, Queen Elizabeth's predecessors personally exercised supreme executive, legislative and judicial powers. By the end of the last century all the sovereign's

political power was terminated and the Queen must now accede to Parliament's wishes and be an impartial head of state.

The Queen was never destined for the throne from birth. Her father and mother were the Duke and Duchess of York, and it was never thought likely that they would become King George VI and Queen Elizabeth. Her uncle, the popular Prince of Wales, was destined to succeed to the throne. That he would abdicate to marry the woman he loved

was a dramatic gesture never imagined by the family of the uncrowned King Edward VIII. Elizabeth, therefore, never anticipated being trained for the life of a monarch. She was 'Lilibet', a cheerful child, not too serious, enjoying a privileged existence in a smart Mayfair house, outdoor fun at Royal Lodge, Windsor, and playing among the heather at Birkhall near Balmoral.

All this changed for her and her sister Margaret when they were ten and six years old respectively. Their uncle David gave up his throne and their father had to step into his shoes. From then on life took on a more serious aspect because now Elizabeth had to be trained to become a sovereign. Private lessons became more purposeful and a little of her light-heartedness disappeared as she became more involved in protocol and learning about the affairs of state. Until then she and Princess Margaret had grown up in a blissfully happy home, without any of the pressures of impending responsibility that, for example, Prince Charles has had to face.

Elizabeth spent her teenage years during the austerity of the Second World War, when she soon learned about the obligations of being a monarch as she shared the dangers of the Blitz in London with her father's subjects, and toured the war-torn areas of the country with her parents. When she was old enough she joined the

Taken on the occasion of their marriage on 20th November, 1947, the photographs on the opposite page are of the young Princess Elizabeth and Lieutenant Philip Mountbatten (Baron).

His Royal Highness Prince Charles was born on the 14th November, 1948 and the first picture of the family together above far left was taken when the baby was nineteen weeks old (Baron).

After the christening of Prince Charles, four Royal generations feature together above left. King George VI is standing behind his mother, Queen Mary and his daughter, Princess Elizabeth who nurses the baby prince (Baron).

The Royal couple are shown left in 1950 with Prince Charles and Princess Anne (Baron).

ROYAL FAMILY

Army, wearing khaki as an officer in the Auxiliary Territorial Service, the predecessor of today's Women's Royal Army Corps.

The Queen was only twenty-five when her father died in February 1952. He died while Princess Elizabeth and Prince Philip were in Kenya on the first leg of a royal tour of East Africa, Australia and New Zealand. His death did not come as a surprise to the princess and the rest of the family.

He had been ill for more than three years, a grim piece of information that had been kept quiet from his subjects and the world at large. In March 1949

he underwent an operation to improve the circulation in his right foot. Two years later, the Queen Mother and the two princesses had confirmation of their worst fears – King George, a heavy smoker, had a cancerous growth in his left lung.

Surgeons did their best and after an operation the King seemed to make a bright recovery. It was not to last. Less than a year later the illness took its toll. Few who were present or saw newsreel and newspaper photographs will for-

The Queen takes part above and above right in the pageantry and tradition which inevitably plays a large and important role in the calendar of the Royal Family.

In 1960, Her Majesty was photographed right by Cecil Beaton, who also took the splendid picture far right of the Queen and Prince Philip.

get the haggard expression on his face as he waved farewell to his eldest daughter and her husband at London Airport when they set off on their world tour. It was a harsh winter's day. He was so ill that he should not have ventured out – yet it almost seems as if he sensed it might be the last time he would see his 'Lilibet'.

A week later he was at the royal estate of Sandringham, enjoying one of his favourite sports – shooting pheasant. At the end of the day he had dinner with his queen, listened to radio reports of Princess Elizabeth's tour in Africa, then had a cup of cocoa while he read a magazine. He went to bed and died in his sleep from a coronary thrombosis. The King was found dead by one of the valets, who drew back the curtains, turned round to say 'good morning' and faced a stilled body. At 56 years of age the man who had never sought the throne, yet became one of Britain's greatest loved monarchs, had gone.

'Long live the Queen' was the shout from town hall steps throughout the Commonwealth as the official announcement of his death was made. A new Elizabethan Age had begun, four hundred years after the previous magnificent period in British history during the reign of the first Queen Elizabeth.

Above the muddy pond where lion and zebra drink in the Aberdare Forest of Kenya there was no rejoicing for a new golden age. Princess Elizabeth was told that she was now Queen after she and the Prince had spent the night in the hotel on stilts which was known as 'Treetops'. A father had died and all his daughter wanted to do was to cry and mourn his passing, comforted by her husband. The harshness of the responsibility of her new role, however, became clear to her as the day progressed.

From Treetops they returned to a nearby royal hunting lodge at Sagana where they had been spending a few days' holiday. By the time they arrived news agency reports were confirmed by official telegrams and messages from London that made clear where her duties now lay. They were couched in courtly politeness, but it was evident that she was not to suffer her grief in private like a member of any other family. She was now Elizabeth the Queen, and, as such, she must be seen to rule as soon as possible. The public needed evidence that the majesty of

ROYAL FAMILY

monarchy would continue. The new Queen Elizabeth II therefore, in the days before Concorde, made a tiring night and day flight back to England with Prince Philip.

All the Royal Family carry around with them while they are on tour, at home or overseas, a suitcase which they hope they will never have to open containing mourning clothes. Smartly tailored, they are included in the luggage ready to wear should they have to dash back to London on receiving the news of a royal or statesman's death. The proprieties of public death have to be observed and Elizabeth changed on the last leg of her flight into a long black coat and cockaded black hat from that neglected suitcase.

As if to signify the loneliness of her new role, she walked down the aircraft steps by herself – a shy, almost timorous young woman, who had left London only eight days earlier as a carefree wife, and now returned to face the task of being one of the most significant personalities of the twentieth century. Waiting to greet her at the bottom of the aircraft steps was her Prime Minister, Winston Churchill. Elizabeth had always hoped that she would not have to take the throne so soon after her marriage. She and Philip had been married for four years and were just beginning to settle down to enjoy the marvellous experience of being a young couple with children. She had wanted to go through the experience of being the wife of a naval officer, a mother of two growing children, and build a home and family life, just like any other woman, before accepting the duties of the Crown.

The fact that she had to assume royal duties so early in life, depriving her of so much of the freedom that others in their twenties can expect, has influenced, to a certain degree, the Queen's attitude towards Prince Charles. She knows what it is like to have to bear so early the monarchial chains of office. For this reason she wishes that Charles should have the chance to marry, set up a home and lead an undisturbed domestic life before it is his turn to take over the throne.

Prince Charles frequently says that it could be as long as thirty or forty years before he becomes king, pointing out how healthy and keen for the job his mother still is. Waiting for so long would mean Charles reaching his sixties before he has the chance to rule.

The Queen and her advisers would, nevertheless, like the heir to the throne to still be young and full of vigour when his time to don the kingly mantle arrives. Should the Queen, as some people say, decide to abdicate in favour of her son, it will certainly not be until he has had a better chance than she had of being just a parent first and a monarch second.

Her full duties began in earnest sixteen months after her return to England as Queen, when Elizabeth was crowned in Westminster Abbey

The striking portrait of the Queen at the age of forty-three above was painted by Pietro Annigoni

Her Majesty's official birthday is always held on a Saturday in June and marked by the Trooping the Colour Ceremony. The Queen is seen right on this spectacular and colourful occasion, which never fails to draw huge crowds.

ROYAL FAMILY

on a rainy June 2, 1953. The country, which was beginning to recover from the Second World War, still had the wealth and might of a major power and the coronation gave Britain the opportunity to demonstrate her imperial vigour to the world. More than ten thousand servicemen – a quarter of them 'soldiers of the Queen' from the Commonwealth – marched in the coronation procession. Two thousand

bandsmen, making up nearly fifty bands, provided the music. Fellow sovereigns and rulers from all over the globe came to pay tribute to the girlish figure who was now the head of the greatest group of nations in history. A hundred thousand people braved the wet weather along the streets. Such was the length of the procession that it took 45 minutes to pass any one spot.

On the morning of the coronation there had been ructions at Buckingham Palace, because four-year-old Charles was allowed to attend the ceremony while his sister, two years younger, was told that she would have to stay at home. There were tantrums, but the Queen insisted that Anne was too young to go to Westminster Abbey. As it turned out, the four-hour long service proved too much for the satin-suited Charles, anyway. He watched the crowning standing alongside his grandmother, but then he became im-

patient and noisy, so he was obliged to leave early.

When the Queen and Prince Philip returned to the palace they were hugged and kissed by the children, who were greeting their 'mum and dad' – not a newly invested sovereign and her consort. Princess Anne, wearing a pretty white party frock was allowed to take part – at last – in some of the day's excitement. She and

Charles came onto the balcony to wave to the crowds and see the fly-past by the Royal Air Force. The family of Elizabeth and Philip had become truly royal. They were under great pressure in a changing world and faced public curiosity even into their most private moments.

In the years since her coronation the demands on the Queen have been enormous. With jet aircraft speeding up

global travel, she, together with Prince Philip, has undertaken more tours abroad than any previous monarch. She has had to maintain stately calm and continuity during a period of industrial, social and political change. She has had to ensure the smooth transition of a colonial empire into a Commonwealth and yet, despite this hectic life, she has achieved a happy family existence with her husband and

The picture top shows the Queen with Prince Philip, Prince Charles, Princess Anne, Prince Andrew and Prince Edward at the time of her Silver Wedding (Patrick Lichfield). Prince Charles enjoys the fresh air of Balmoral above; Princess Anne and Captain Mark Phillips share a quiet moment above left (Norman Parkinson) and the Queen relaxes at an equestrian event above far left.

ROYAL FAMILY

children.

The Queen best summed up her attitude towards family life when she said

at the time of her silver wedding anniversary: *'A marriage begins by joining man and wife together, but this relationship between two people, however deep at the time, needs to develop and mature with the passing years. For that it must be held firm in the web of the family relationships, between parents and children, between grandparents and grandchildren, between cousins, aunts and uncles. If I am asked today what I think about family life after 25 years of marriage I can answer with simplicity and conviction. I am for it.'*

In the grounds of Balmoral Castle, the Queen savours a moment of peace left (Patrick Lichfield) and the Queen Mother above displays that much loved smile.

On Jubilee day overleaf, the Queen accepts with delight, flowers and congratulations from devoted crowds.

ENGLAND

So much has been written about England; there is no other country which has been so eulogised throughout the centuries; and yet Keats' gentle lyricism belies the patriotic passion that lies behind that lovely verse and encapsulates the fierce pride that dwells within the English breast.

This mongrel breed, which has so readily absorbed the cultures and languages of a good many foreign invaders, embellished them and made them its own, will stoutly defend the amorphous 'Englishness' of an Englishman – for to be English does not necessarily mean that one has to be of pure-bred English stock (indeed few are!) – it is rather a passion for the country itself: its *green and pleasant land*; the vagaries of the weather, and the sure belief that no other country on earth can be such a 'commodious' place in which to live.

It is not surprising that this tiny country reveals such a rich diversity of landscape, for although comparatively young on the geological time scale, its complex structure, spanning 600,000,000 years, illustrates almost every stage of geological history, from the oldest igneous rocks of the extreme west and north to the recent alluvial soils of reclaimed fenland in East Anglia. Some of the most splendid examples can be seen in the striking shoreline cliff structures, particularly those of the ancient granite precipices at Land's End, succeeding through the vari-coloured sandstones and multi-aged limestones to the dazzling white chalk bluffs of the South Downs, and the rugged desert sandstones of the northern Pennines, with their wild, bleak moors, that split the north of England longitudinally.

The earliest known human remains in Britain, dating back approximately a quarter of a million years, are the fragments of a human skull found in a gravel pit by the lower Thames at Swanscombe, and the Swanscombe

Washed by crested breakers, Godrevy Island Lighthouse left stands sentinel in St Ives Bay.

ENGLAND

Man, as he is now referred to, is recognised as one of the direct ancestors of Homo sapiens. By the time the North Sea had been formed (about 6,000 B.C.) and the mainland link with France severed, the island was populated by hunters who were also to become skilled in the arts of carpentry and fishing, and who were later joined by foreign immigrants, including a short, swarthy-complexioned Mediterranean people who settled in the Cotswolds and on the chalk hills, about 2,400 B.C. These New Stone Age farmers, the first in Britain, were responsible for the building of the long, narrow burial mounds, or barrows, predominantly conspicuous on the chalk downlands, and the megalithic tombs that were built by the settlers along the western coast.

By the end of the New Stone Age, Britain's most famous and awe-inspiring megalithic monument – Stonehenge – was under construction, with the completion of the outer circular ditch and bank, a ring of 56 pits known as the Aubrey Holes just inside the bank, and the Heel stone which stands 256 feet from the centre circle on the avenue leading from the north-eastern break in the bank. During the second millennium, about 1800 B.C., the Beaker Folk arrived from Holland and the Rhineland, at the dawn of the Bronze Age. They played a major role, not only in the second stage of development at Stonehenge with the transportation of the pillars of igneous

rock or 'bluestones' from the Prescelly Mountains in South-West Wales, but also in the creation of the fascinating Avebury Stone Circle – some one hundred sarsen stones of huge dimensions – which ring the picturesque Wiltshire Village. Stonehenge was later remodelled during the 15th century B.C. when about eighty huge blocks of sarsen were brought from the Marl-

borough Downs to form a unique circle, with its carefully shaped lintels and trilithons, and inner horseshoe formation, the remains of which can still be seen today.

From the brooding mystery of Stonehenge to the northern limit of Roman occupation – Hadrian's Wall – England has a wealth of fascinating history which is woven into the very

fabric of its hills and dales, bustling towns and cities, sleepy villages and sea-washed shores and, in spite of the fact that over the centuries the landscape has been significantly changed by its occupants, the basic structure of life in scattered groups, whether in modern cities or close-knit villages, perpetuates the picture of England as a pastoral country that still persists even in the 20th century.

The South West

Rocky coastlines pounded by the spuming white foam of Atlantic breakers and a northern coast of soft, sandy beaches contrasted with the calmer waters of the South West's famed 'Riviera', where sparkling blue waters lap the tiny coves and bays that lie on its opposite shore, and, between, the wild, wind-blown moors, rolling hills and steep river valleys – South West England is steeped in centuries of romantic legend. It was amid this land of sudden mists that King Arthur and his Knights of the Round Table were said to have kept their court; it was this land that nurtured the Elizabethan sea-adventurers – Raleigh, Drake and Hawkins – whose tall-masted ships sailed the Spanish Main and the routes to the 'New World'; the land that inspired writers and poets, such as the novelist Daphne Du Maurier, who wove her story of romance and intrigue, 'Frenchman's Creek', around the spectacular scenery of its crenellated shoreline.

Until modern times Cornwall was virtually isolated from the rest of the country, the Tamar River forming a formidable barrier with neighbouring Devon as it slices across the peninsula from Woolley Barrow to the Plymouth Sound, until Brunel's elegant Victorian bridge at Saltash carried the railway across the river. This feeling of remoteness is nowhere better illustrated than

Beyond the rugged outline of Land's End, the furthest point west on the mainland of England, Longships Lighthouse above left perches on a lonely Atlantic rock. According to legend St Michael's Mount left is part of the lost kingdom of Lyonesse, where once King Arthur's knights rode. Gwithian's Lighthouse appears on the horizon right beyond Gwithian Sands, while overleaf the famous granite mass of Land's End tumbles into the sea at the end of Penwith Peninsula.

ENGLAND

in the lonely Longships Lighthouse, standing beyond the granite grandeur of Land's End, at the tip of the Penwith Peninsula, where countless ships have perished on the merciless rocks. The shoreline is peppered with picturesque fishing villages and yachting resorts, each with its own distinctive charm and mystery, that now play host to the vast numbers of tourists who flock, each summer, to spend their leisure time here.

From The Lizard, the southernmost part of England, with its soaring cliffs and pinnacles of rock reaching down to Lizard Point, up to Camborne, once the centre of Cornwall's tin mining industry, and beyond, the old pump houses, once so necessary to the miners to guard against the flooding with which they were constantly threatened, still dot the landscape. Cliff-top churches perch atop the craggy bluffs that overlook the sand and shingle beaches; cob and thatch cottages line the winding country lanes of Devon amid the rich, red-soiled farming land, and slate and granite cots hug the inland, windswept moors. Stirring reminders of past history, such as Pendennis Castle at Falmouth; Restormel Castle, close to Lostwithiel; the Methodist 'Cathedral' at Gwennap Pit, where John Wesley preached in the mid-18th century and St Michael's Mount, opposite Penzance, which, according to legend, is part of the lost kingdom of Lyonesse, where King Arthur's knights once rode, kindle the imagination, while the bleak and wild moors of Bodmin and Dartmoor are renowned for their rugged, isolated beauty.

Cornwall's cathedral city and administrative centre is Truro, noted for

Cornwall possesses a wealth of picturesque villages such as East Looe above facing page and Polperro above and overleaf. In the hamlet of Codgwith above left a local fisherman proudly dislays his catch but the tourists have discovered St Ives facing page below, where much of the fishing is now done by holiday-makers.

Legend has it that the huge granite rocks near Newquay top were stepping stones of the giant Beduthan and at Launceston left the stone ramparts of a 13th-century castle still remain.

ENGLAND

its striking, triple-tiered cathedral which was completed in 1910. For eight centuries the Sees of Cornwall and Devon were united, until the reconstitution of the Cornish See in 1897.

Exeter, in Devon, the South West's major city, and one of England's most historic, contains the remains of one of the largest Roman bath houses ever to be excavated in Britain, as well as a magnificent 14th-century cathedral (thought to be its crowning glory) noted for its two outstanding Norman towers and renowned carved figures on the west front; plus a wealth of fine buildings, mansions, castles and abbeys.

It was from Plymouth, the largest city in the West Country, that the Pilgrim Fathers, aboard the Mayflower, set sail for America in 1620. Here, over three centuries later, in 1966, the city would witness the start of another epic journey, that of Sir Francis Chichester's, as he commenced his successful single-handed voyage around the world.

One of the South West's show-pieces is undoubtedly picturesque Clovelly, lying in a lush, narrow combe between the steep Devon cliffs. Cars are banned from the village and the precipitous main street is almost continually filled with fragrant, colourful flowers. East of sophisticated Torquay, Devon's largest and most famous seaside resort, is spectacular Kent's Cavern, occupied by prehistoric men and animals during the last Ice-Age, and one of the oldest known human dwelling-places in Britain.

It is not surprising that this beautiful region of England, occupied from Neo-

In a lush, narrow combe between steep cliffs, Clovelly left, far left and below is one of the show-places of Devon. Cars are not permitted to enter the village and the cottages lining the steep main street are decked with flowers for most of the year.

Tintagel Castle on the cliffs below left stands on the site of what was once one of King Arthur's strongholds and on a Treen cliff overleaf, 'logan' rock, weighing about 65 tons, 'logs' or rocks, at the slightest touch.

variety of scenery within a compact area, that marks the peculiar mystique of England.

Southern Counties

A great profusion of well-blended beauty and quiet solitude amid pastoral landscapes rich in historic remains, from the neolithic monuments on Salisbury Plain to the elegant Georgian architecture of Bath, clothes the rural loveliness of the Southern Counties.

Surrounded by myth and legend, Glastonbury in Somerset, lying on slopes that incline from the Brue Valley to a 522 ft tor, topped by the fragmented remains of the Benedictine abbey of St Mary, is the cradle of Christianity in Britain. It is said that

lithic times through the Roman invasion, and a bastion of the old Celtic ways, should continue to beckon the artists and writers for whom it has long provided ideal inspiration, as well as the scores of holiday-makers, who at the end of their stay, are loathe to forsake its charms, for its diversity of landscape, blessed with the country's mildest climate, affords a distinctive

Left St Ives and the quiet seclusion of Polperro right.

ENGLAND

when St Joseph of Arimathea came to the town, bringing with him the chalice used at the Last Supper, he leant in prayer on his thorn staff, which immediately took root, indicating that he should stay and found a religious house. The winter-flowering Glastonbury thorn-tree that sprang from the original root on Wirrall Hill is purported to have been hacked down by a Roundhead during the Civil War, but a thorn-tree in the abbey grounds is claimed to be a cutting from it. According to Arthurian legend, King Arthur, whose Camelot is thought to be Cadbury Castle, near Sutton Mentis, and

his Queen, Guinevere, were re-interred in the abbey, and the Holy Grail, brought by Joseph, which Arthur's knights sought, is believed to be buried below the Chalice Spring on Glastonbury Tor.

Considered to be the loveliest part of Somerset, the undulating, wooded Quantock Hills have close affiliations with the poets Coleridge and Wordsworth, who strolled amid the dark, tangled woods and heather-covered moorland, whilst Blackmore's evocative 'Lorna Doone' conjures images of the lonely Mendip Hills, rent by the towering limestone cliffs of the awe-inspiring Cheddar Gorge.

Facing the Severn estuary and the southern part of the Cotswolds Hills, the county of Avon contains the spectacular Avon Gorge, spanned by Brunel's remarkable Clifton Suspension Bridge towering 245 ft above the Avon River's high-water level and affording some of the finest panoramic views of the gorge and surrounding countryside. Bristol, combining old and new in pleasing proportions, has been a thriving commercial port since the 10th century. It was from this important city that John Cabot set sail

A cobbled street in Clovelly *left* falls steeply away towards the sea, while *far left*, set in its fine patchwork landscape, lies Salcombe, the country's southernmost resort and a noted yachting centre.

Dartmouth *right* has been an important harbour since the Roman era and Seaton *above right* has a mile-long beach which is timeless in its beauty. Yet inland Devon is equally fascinating: Buckland-in-the-Moor *top* must be one of the most photographed villages in England, and Bampton *above* draws the crowds to its annual pony fair.

ENGLAND

in discovery of North America and Newfoundland, in 1497, in the 100-ton *Matthew*, and in 1552 was founded the Society of Merchant Venturers who played such an important role in the development of the mighty Empire.

Around the Roman baths of the settlement of Aquae Sulis, chosen for the valuable mineral waters that originate in the Eastern Mendips, grew the beautiful city that was to take their name and which was to come to the full flowering of its grace and charm during Georgian times. Although prosperous throughout the Middle Ages, Bath's fame is closely associated with the high society of the Regency period, when the talented dandy, Beau Nash, presided over the pump-room balls and elegant assemblies, so delightfully described in Jane Austen's 19th-century novels.

As famous as the prehistoric monuments that rise from the vast stillness of Wiltshire's Salisbury Plain, New

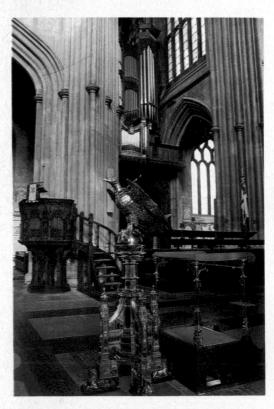

Magnificent stained glass windows adorn the east end of the Chapel of Our Lady far right in Exeter Cathedral – possibly the greatest glory of one of the most historic cities of Britain.

Bath in Somerset, which began in AD44 as an important Roman settlement, is also a city of great historical interest. At its heart stands the magnificent abbey shown on this page.

Sarum, or Salisbury, built at the confluence of four river valleys, and one of the loveliest of England's many cathedral cities, is famed for its magnificent centrepiece, set amid a splendid conglomeration of varying architectural styles – the resplendent mediaeval cathedral with its majestic, soaring spire and graceful cloisters, eulogised by Trollope. Among its many treasures is one of the four original copies of Magna Carta which is housed in the library over the East Walk. West of the city lie the valleys of the Wylye and the Nadder, divided by the forest downlands of Grovely Wood and the Great Ridge, along which can be traced the route of a Roman road as it swings west towards Bath.

Dorset is rich farming country, famous for its rolling pastures providing its creamy milk and delicious cheeses. Immortalised by the great English novelist and observer of rural life, Thomas Hardy, who was born in

An abbey has presided over Bath these pages since Saxon times but the original building was almost entirely rebuilt by Bishop Montagu in the 17th century and further 19th-century restorations did much to influence its present form.

The Roman settlement Aquae Sulis grew up around the warm springs which made Bath the most celebrated of English spas and today the Great Roman Bath left survives as an impressive monument to Roman Britain.

ENGLAND

the- picturesque hamlet of Bock-hampton, the pastoral scenes provided memorable backgrounds to many of his famous novels. Belying the un-disturbed, rural tranquillity, however, is a dramatic coastline, particularly impressive in the crumbling, limestone cliffs which culminate in Durdle Door, a massive, natural arch of Purbeck stone that guards the entrance to Man O' War Bay.

England, as a maritime nation, has always had strong associations with the sea. Nowhere is this more evident than along the coast of Hampshire; Buckler's Hard may seem an unlikely setting today, with horses grazing on the wide, main street, but it was here, in the 18th century, that many of the

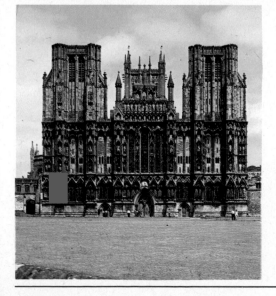

Wells above and above left, in Somerset, is particularly famous for its cathedral, begun in the 12th century. Its West Front left, originally embellished with nearly 400 statues of saints, angels and prophets, is one of the finest in Britain.

Only fragments remain of Glastonbury's 13th-century abbey far left, the last of a series on this site. Legend tells how Joseph of Arimathea came here to convert the English. As he leant upon his staff to pray, it took root, indicating that the saint should stay and found a religious house.

ships were built which were to sail under the command of Nelson in the Napoleonic War. This naval tradition is carried on, and brought up to date, at Portsmouth, with its great dockyards and training schools, and a poignant reminder of its past is Nelson's flagship, the Victory, berthed among sheds of red brick and concrete in the dockyard itself, on board which this most famous of England's naval heroes died.

Synonymous with Hampshire is the New Forest – the famed royal hunting ground which was a favourite of King John – its vast woodland teeming with a variety of wildlife including the celebrated New Forest pony. Today this oldest of the great forests of

ENGLAND

England, covering 145 square miles, is administered by a special group of officials, called Verderers, who are responsible for maintaining law and order, in addition to the welfare of the many animals which inhabit the preserve.

Separated from the Hampshire coastline, with its wealth of fine resorts, by the Solent and Spithead, lies the delightful holiday island of the Isle of Wight, a favourite of the Victorians since Queen Victoria endorsed its qualities. It was in the royal country retreat of Osborne House in East Cowes, that Queen Victoria died in 1901.

South-East England

Trim meadows and wide-ribboned rivers are woven into the texture of this prominent corner of England as it juts boldly into the English Channel, whilst its gleaming, white chalk cliffs are backed by the rolling Sussex Downs, littered with a host of ruined fortifications that bear witness to successive armies of invaders who, throughout the centuries, have left their marks on this, their first foothold on the land they set out to conquer.

The Romans succeeded in subjugating the country to their laws for a while, but then abandoned it and went back to their homeland. William and his Normans, as every schoolboy knows, landed at, or near, Hastings, then made their way inland to Battle to face a weary army. Tricked by the Normans into believing that they were retreating, the Saxons chased them in disarray and paid dearly for their mistake. Their king was dead and the country had a new ruler. The last successful invasion of England had become history! Whenever defences are breached they tend to be strengthened by the conquerors, to ensure that they cannot be caught out by others intent on following their example and this, largely, accounts for the great wealth of castles around the coast, such as the particularly fine examples at Arundel and Bodiam.

Sussex is by no means only a county of historic castles and battlefields, *A graceful 19th-century spire rising 285 feet from the ground, rests on the fine 13th-century tower of St Mary Redcliffe in Bristol below left.*

Bath was made a showpiece for 18th-century architecture, by architects such as John Wood the Younger, who was responsible for the Royal Crescent bottom, an elegant open design of thirty houses in a sweeping semi-ellipse, and Robert Adam, who designed the Florentine, shop-lined Pulteney Bridge below and right. A tribute to more recent design, the Severn Suspension Bridge overleaf, opened in 1966, carries traffic across the river estuary.

ENGLAND

however. The South Downs are full of natural beauty, and wooded hills and valleys, delightful villages and fine coastal resorts are part of the area's enormous variety. The picturesque old town of Rye, once a lively port, but now left stranded by the receding sea, still retains the character it had when it was a notorious haunt of smugglers. Eastbourne, at one time a small fishing village, is still the elegant resort that the 7th Duke of Devonshire designed in 1834, and nearby Beachy Head, the highest cliff on the south coast, towering 534 ft above the sea, still attracts countless visitors who can, on a clear day, glimpse the Isle of Wight to the west and Dungeness to the east. Brighton, possibly the most well-known resort on the Sussex coast, with its fairy-tale Royal Pavilion, is an intriguing confection of graceful Georgian houses, gaudy sea-side paraphernalia, bracing sea-air and delightful old shops and houses that line the narrow, picturesque 'Lanes'. Just west of the cathedral town of Chichester lies one of the major Roman relics in Britain, at Fishbourne, where excavations have revealed an important

At Cheddar Gorge right rugged cliffs, probably cut out by a stream now subterranean, soar to about 450 feet.

Throughout the West Country, wherever the tracks of the railways lead and there are rivers or gorges to be crossed, it is difficult to escape the work of Isambard Kingdom Brunel, a remarkable engineer who displayed enormous skill and imagination, in construction and in the elegance of his design.

The imposing Clifton Suspension Bridge left, above and right, built by Brunel in 1864, spans the River Avon at a point where it flows between steep limestone cliffs. By night its illuminations impress themselves dramatically on the shadowy outlines of the surrounding rocks.

ENGLAND

Roman palace occupied during the 2nd and 3rd centuries A.D., while south-east of the Black Down, the highest point in Sussex, stands the mediaeval town of Petworth and the magnificent mansion of Petworth House, with its superb art collection that includes a series of exquisite Turner paintings of the local landscapes that the artist loved so well.

Although to many people Surrey conjures up the image of one vast London commuter land, the county has, nevertheless, managed to retain much of its natural beauty in generous open spaces, such as Box Hill, one of the South East's best known beauty spots on the North Downs and a popular picnic area as long ago as the reign of Charles II, and in its charming villages, rich in historic interest. The very banks of the River Thames, as it winds its way through the countryside, endorse the fact. Runnymede saw the granting by King John of the draft of Magna Carta in 1215 and the site now stands in National Trust Property. Historic Richmond, so named by Henry VII to commemorate his original title of Duke of Richmond, stands on the slopes of a hill from the top of which may be seen a famous and most beautiful view of the river. Nearby Kingston-upon-Thames has been a royal borough for over 1,100 years. Outside the Guildhall may be seen the 'King's Stone' on which several Saxon Kings are said to have been crowned. The county also contains some of the country's finest botanical gardens: Kew Gardens which was landscaped by 'Capability' Brown, with its great Palm House and whimsical Pagoda; the Royal Horticultural Society's delightful 300-acre experimental gardens at Wisley, and Winkworth Arboretum's superb woodland acres.

Often referred to as 'the garden of England', the fertile soil of Kent has supported orchards and vineyards

Among the many charming Cotswold villages with their characteristic stone houses, Upper Slaughter in Gloucestershire far right is one of the most frequently visited, but it was Bibury right that William Morris described as the most beautiful village in England. Apparently oblivious to time, the River Windrush still flows beside the main street in Bourton-on-the-Water above right and above far right.

since Roman times. Hops, too, have been grown in the county for over four thousand years and today the hop fields cover some 10,000 acres, mainly in the Medway Valley and in a belt from Faversham to Canterbury, where traditional, conical-roofed oast-houses for hop drying, are a familiar and pretty part of the rural scene. Beyond the rich valleys the North Downs stretch towards the Kent coastline, peppered with myriad coastal ports that once presented the first line of defence against invaders, culminating in the famed white cliffs of Dover as they preside over the narrowest part of the English Channel. For centuries Dover has played a major role in British history, and the road, from this busiest of English passenger ports, to Canterbury – the birthplace of Christianity in Saxon England, to where mediaeval pilgrims trudged the ancient trackway of the 'Pilgrims Way', so eloquently represented by Chaucer, that they might worship at the shrine of the murdered Thomas à Becket in the long,

Unspoilt houses and settings have made Gloucestershire villages like Naunton above left, Buckland above and Upper Slaughter overleaf the resort of those in search of old world tranquillity. At Hidcote left, a lovely manor house has been carefully preserved. The ancient city of Gloucester has a fine Norman to Early Perpendicular cathedral above right and Tewkesbury is famous for its abbey right, topped by a beautiful Norman tower.

ENGLAND

grey cathedral that dominates the city and which is the Mother Church of Anglicans throughout the world – still follows the route of the Roman Watling Street.

The Home Counties

Fanning westwards and north of London, the rich diversity of landscape that marks the five 'Home Counties' of England is due, primarily, to the three hill regions of the Chilterns, the Cotswolds and the Berkshire Downs, and

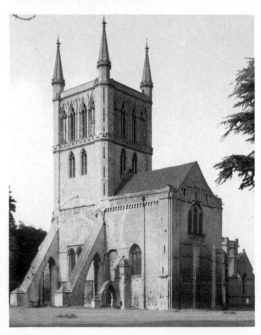

Churches form an essential part of the tradition and atmosphere of English life. The tranquil village churches of Overbury top left, Snowshill left and Naunton overleaf; the abbeys at Pershore above or Tewkesbury right; and Chipping Camden's impressive church top – all are vital monuments to religious and architectural history.

ENGLAND

the meandering rivers, notably the Thames and the Great Ouse, that wind through this fascinating area suffused in ancient history.

From its source in the Cotswolds the orderly Thames flows through Oxfordshire and Berkshire, its lush water-meadows marking the counties' boundary. To the south of the river, on the bold escarpment of the Berkshire Downs bordering the fertile, flat farmlands, looms the 374 ft figure of the White Horse, after which the Vale is named. Myth and controversy sur-

Gloucestershire and Worcestershire are renowned for their undisturbed rural charm: Lower Slaughter left, Overbury Court centre left, Chedworth below, Broadway below right and St John's Lock at Lechlade right are only some of their many tranquil corners. At Evesham bottom left a fine Perpendicular bell tower remains among the old abbey ruins.

round this gigantic form which, some claim, was cut into the chalk in Saxon times, while others assert that the art-style is similar to that of the Iron Age Celts and believe that the figure is representative of their goddess Epona, protectress of horses. The ancient tracks of the Icknield Way and Ridge Way, as they cross the lovely Berkshire Downs, also give some indication of how far back in antiquity people have occupied the area. Although the county is punctuated with a wealth of historic mansions, the most celebrated is undoubtedly that of Windsor Castle

as it dominates the leafy banks of the glorious Thames. Built by William the Conqueror, and improved and embellished by succeeding monarchs, the castle first became a royal home during the reign of Henry I. Contained within its soft grey walls is some of the finest architecture in England, notably in the magnificent St George's Chapel.

Where the Thames meets the Cherwell, in the Upper Thames Basin, and is known as the Isis, rise the honey-coloured stone buildings and 'dreaming spires' of Oxfordshire's crowning glory and its ancient seat of learning –

ENGLAND

Oxford – part of England's cultural heritage. It was during the 8th century that the city was formed with the founding of St Frideswide's nunnery. By 1214 a university was established and before the close of the 13th century the four colleges of Balliol, Merton, St Edmund Hall and University had been instituted. Over the succeeding centuries other historic colleges swelled their ranks, to where those with propensity would seek the dissemination of knowledge, within those hallowed walls.

Dramatically rent by the low chalk ridge of the Chilterns, the face of Buckinghamshire presents one of England's richest agricultural regions, Creslow

Great Field, on its northern profile, and a countryside of beechwoods and bluebells, mossy banks and silver streams on its southern. It was in this county, so full of history, in an old stone church surrounded by a huge, gilded ball, which perches on a hilltop in West Wycombe Park, that the members of the notorious Hell Fire Club, an 18th-century group of gamblers and rakes, met to plot their witchcraft orgies. At Jordan, near Beaconsfield, can be seen beams that formed part of the Pilgrim Father's 'Mayflower'; Penn was the home of William Penn, the founder of Pennsylvania in the 'New World', and in Chalfont St Giles stands the mellow cottage which was inhabited by Milton when he fled London to escape the

ENGLAND

An 18th-century tower *below* overlooks Broadway from the top of Fish Hill. Springtime brings daffodils to the churchyard in Upton Bishop *bottom* and autumn lends its distinctive shades to Symonds Yat and the River Wye near Coppet's Hill *left*. Overleaf the same river continues its winding course.

The graceful church facing page *far left* stands in Evesham, a town which also boasts the half-timbered gateway on an original Norman stone base *bottom left*. Holland House in Cropthorne *top left* is characteristic of the thatched Worcestershire houses, while the picturesque half-timbered houses of Tewkesbury *centre left* form a calm Gloucestershire scene.

ENGLAND

Great Plague in 1665. Oddly enough, Buckingham is not the county seat, although it once was. It was given the title by Alfred the Great, but lost it in 1725, when the honour was transferred to Aylesbury. The county of Buckinghamshire reflects so admirably the fascination of English history in that it is made up of so many small incidents, as well as the great and the obvious.

From Buckinghamshire the Great Ouse curves its way through the green pasturelands of north Bedfordshire, a peaceful region that has remained unspoilt by the passage of time. Straddling the great river is the county town of Bedford, with its attractive conglomerate of varying architectural styles, closely associated with John Bunyan – of 'The Pilgrim's Progress' fame – who spent over half his life in the town (although a great deal of it in Bedford Jail!). This beautiful county displays its most varied scenery in its southernmost tip, where the wind-blown Dunstable Downs, affording views over nine counties, provide an ideal launching ground for gliders. High on the Downs is sited the unique and internationally-known zoo of Whipsnade, where visitors do not even need to step out of their cars to see many of the animals! Here, too, is the magnificent stately home of Woburn, with its famous Wildlife Park.

Picturesque Hertfordshire, although bisected by arterial roads since Roman times, is one of the country's prettiest counties. Leafy lanes wind and loop through the grassy hills and steep little valleys of the rural countryside, where half-timbered houses and thatched-roofed cottages huddle in numerous scattered villages. Hertfordshire, too, has its rich share of history. The city of St Albans dates back 2,000 years, and is the third important town on the site. Its magnificent abbey, originally built by the Saxons to commemorate Britain's first Christian martyr, St Alban, was rebuilt by the Normans and later enlarged, in the 13th century.

Herefordshire on these pages incorporates another very beautiful part of England.

The village of Castle Combe overleaf is one of the prettiest in Wiltshire.

ENGLAND

West of the city stands the splendid, ruined remains of Verulamium, one of the finest Roman towns in England, exhibiting a fine example of a huge theatre which dates from the mid-2nd century A.D., in addition to important remains that are housed in a nearby museum. It was in the Old Palace, adjoining the splendid Jacobean mansion of Hatfield House, that Queen Elizabeth I spent much of her childhood, while the impressive grounds of Knebworth House, the family home of the Lyttons, have in recent years, become famous as the annual venue of internationally-known 'pop star' concerts.

Eastern Counties

The rump of England astride the Wash, its patchwork farmlands forming an autumnal-hued counterpane across the landscape, has for centuries accommodated numerous invaders who swept in from the sea. Its spacious pasturelands, unforgettably captured on canvas by the great artist Constable, have close associations with some of England's most influential names: it was the land that Boudicca ruled; the birthplace of Oliver Cromwell, Thomas Clarkson and Elizabeth Fry, while through the halls of its beautiful university – Cambridge – have passed a succession of writers who have left an indelible mark on English literature.

Essex is a county of immense contrasts, from the great forested acres of Epping that border the sprawling metropolis of Greater London, through the bustle of industry of the Thames-side area where the bright lights of Southend-on-Sea beckon Londoners to their favourite seaside resort, to the coastal belt of reclaimed marshland that stretches from Shoeburyness to the Blackwater Estuary and includes Foulness, the largest island in the Thames Estuary; its lonely territory playing host, during the winter months, to an estimated 10,000 Brent Geese after they have flown south from their Arctic breeding grounds. The mud-flats and winding creeks, with which this part of the coast abounds, has provided ideal con-ditions for the oysters that are produced here, and the ancient city of Colchester, the heart of the trade, traditionally holds an annual oyster feast that is quite unique.

Along the crumbling coastline of

On a bend in the River Wye, Ross-on-Wye *top* stands against a cloud-hung sky, while *above* the spire of Salisbury Cathedral, the highest in England, rises from the 'water meadows' of the Avon. On Salisbury Plain *left* the sun sets behind the giant prehistoric stone circle of Stonehenge, and *right* the Avebury Stone Circle rings the village of Avebury.

The great Renaissance house of Longleat was built in 1556 by Robert Smythson for Sir John Thynne. It has fine state rooms and art treasures, among them the salon *left*, the drawing room *above left*, the grand staircase *above*, the state dining room *right* and the dress corridor *below*.

Mossy white cliffs drop sharply away to the sea near Lulworth overleaf.

ENGLAND

Suffolk stands Dunwich, one of the most evocative of East Anglia's villages – once the Roman town of Sitomagus and a prosperous trading port with France – which has now largely vanished below the sea. Although little is left of this once-thriving town, devastated by a storm in the 14th century, the sight of its ruined priory and desolate shingle beach beneath the still eroding cliffs fosters an unaccountable emotional experience that is quite uncanny. Numerous writers and artists, including Edward FitzGerald, the translator of 'The Rubáiyát of Omar Khayyám', drew inspiration amid its tragic haunts. It is in the churchyard at Boulge, in the open farmlands of central Suffolk, that FitzGerald lies buried – beneath scented roses that flower from a seed of a tree on the grave of Omar Khayyám and sent from Naishapur. For most people it would be impossible to divorce the Suffolk that we see today from the country that John Constable painted and which was his home. He was born in the village of East Bergholt

The village of Corfe Castle above left and facing page is dominated by a stark, spectacular fortress. Less sinister in its associations, a 15th-century manor is mirrored in a still pool at Athelhampton left, while the River Stour flows under a bridge at Sturminster Newton above. Evening brings renewed meaning to the name of Gold Hill, Shaftesbury's steep, cobbled street overleaf.

ENGLAND

and spent much of his life in painting the countryside which he knew and loved. The River Stour and its locks and banks were especial favourites with him and formed the subjects of many of his best loved works. Possibly the best known, and certainly the one most visited by tourists, is Willy Lott's Cottage at Flatford Mill. Carefully preserved, it remains almost unchanged to this day and looks very much as it must have done to the artist when he sat down by the water with his canvas and brushes.

Norfolk is synonymous with 'The Broads', some 200 miles of open expanses of water with navigable approach channels which, linked with lakes, rivers and waterways – some manmade – make up this delightful area that is seen to advantage from one of the many boats on hire to tourists. Because of the flat, open landscape in this part of the country, wind-driven mills were, for many years, used to grind corn, and it is estimated that there were about one thousand five hundred such mills at work until a century ago. Although their numbers have dwindled since then, enough

Not far from Lulworth lies the sheltered Man o'War Bay right and a huge limestone arch known as Durdle Door, which juts out into the sea above and below far right. Further west along the coast, a lighthouse above warns of potentially hazardous rocks at the renowned Portland Bill.

ENGLAND

remain still to form a picturesque part of the rural landscape. The magnificent cathedral of Holy Trinity in Norwich is the only remaining example in England that conforms to the Apsidal plan, with the Bishop's throne behind the altar, a relic of the days in the early history of Christianity when Roman basilicas were used in the practice of the new religion. While Norwich undoubtedly exhibits a wealth of historic interest, its outskirts too have their charms: Caistor St Edmund, for example, four miles south of the cathedral city, so legend asserts, once formed part of Boudicca's capital.

Hereward the Wake is a legendary figure in English history. A Saxon noble

Viewed from Ballad Down, lush fields roll away to the town of Swanage right, and Bournemouth above far right is another popular Dorset resort. A little further inland, just above the Frome marshes, Wareham above right has retained many of its old buildings, and the small market town of Wimborne Minster above greets the visitor with 'olde worlde' cafés. The well-known resort of Weymouth far right, now a busy port for Channel Island ferries, seems far removed from the town which Thomas Hardy immortalised under the name of Budworth.

ENGLAND

at the time of the occupation of England by William the Conqueror, he resolved to continue the fight against the Normans, and was successful in this for a considerable time – greatly aided by the fact that he took refuge, with his followers, in the Fen country, on the Isle of Ely. The area was almost inaccessible, consisting largely of treacherous marshes, and it is doubtful if any army could ever have reached him, had he not been betrayed by monks. Throughout the centuries that followed work was carried out on the draining of the Fens, but it was not until the 18th century that the Isle of Ely ceased to be an island. Dominating those vast, hedgeless fields is the mediaeval triumph of Ely Cathedral, its unique and magnificent octagonal

To many people Hampshire is synonymous with the New Forest, 90,000 acres of woodland planted over 1,000 years ago to become the royal hunting preserve of William the Conqueror. Set in this magnificent tree-studded landscape, however, are countless charming cottages, this page whilst Lyndhurst left, the administrative centre of the New Forest, defies the main-road traffic with its lovely old buildings.

lantern one of the finest engineering feats of the Middle Ages.

Gentle, undulating hills and peaceful valleys give Cambridgeshire a feeling of space and tranquillity which also permeates its lovely university city of Cambridge. It is a city that requires time spent in exploration to fully appreciate its rare beauty and fascination. The Bridge of Sighs, built in the style of the famous bridge of the same name in Venice, seems not at all out of place in this very English of cities, where punts, instead of gondolas, glide peacefully along the waters of the river that it spans. Renowned colleges, charming churches, quaint little bookshops, and the broad, sweeping lawns of the Backs, are among the many delights that the city has to offer. Perhaps of all the county's most famous literary figures, the name of Rupert Brooke first springs to mind. His poignant 'War Sonnets' earned him fame and popularity during the First World War, and it was to his home in the 'Old Vicarage' at Grantchester, where the poet first lived after leaving King's College, that Brooke dedicated his nos-

ENGLAND

talgic poem, composed in 1912, in a café in Berlin, which epitomises the heartache experienced by many English exiles, particularly during periods of war.

South Midlands

The 'Cockpit of England' is a term often used to describe the South Midlands, at the heart of the country, where a mediaeval cross on the village green at Meriden is said to mark the exact centre of England. This area was witness to a host of battles that more than once shaped the country's destiny, including those of the 'Wars of the Roses' and the dramatic clashes of the Civil War; giving rise to a long list of place names and dates, which history students up and down the country could arguably claim are as agonising to them as they were to the combatants of the field!

Gloucestershire is inevitably linked with the Cotswold Hills that dominate its eastern half, while the mighty Severn River in the west effectively cut the county into two parts for many years, until the opening of the magnificent new suspension bridge, in 1966, gave greater accessibility to the voluptuous Forest of Dean, clothed with the delicious green mantle of an estimated 20 million trees. At the heart of the Severn Valley lies Gloucester, a rich agricultural centre in Roman times: its majestic cathedral containing the second largest mediaeval stained-glass window in the country.

To the west of the Malvern Hills and the lush orchards and market gardens of Worcestershire's Vale of Evesham, lies richly wooded Herefordshire, famed for its apples (accounting for over half of the country's cider production) as well as the white-faced breed of cattle which have been used all over the world to improve other breeds; its historic cathedral city, once the Saxon capital of West Mercia, straddling the meandering Wye River. Even before the Norman conquest Herefordshire, a prime target on the Welsh border, was defended by stout castles against raiders from the Black Mountains which flank the west of the county, and on scenic Symonds Yat can be seen the remains of one of those strongholds, that of Goodrich Castle, which eventually fell to the troops of Oliver Cromwell during the Civil War.

It is hard to believe that the sprawl-

Rivers and waterways bring a particular charm to the English countryside. Past Christchurch Priory below centre right flows the picturesque River Stour, and the River Test winds its way near Longstock bottom right. Lymington right and below, situated on the Lymington River where it flows into the Solent, is a popular and attractive yachting centre.

ing and highly industrialised conurbation of Birmingham – Britain's second largest city with a population well in excess of one million – at the heart of the Midland plain, was, in Shakespeare's day, a thriving market town surrounded by open fields, with the Forest of Arden, north and west of the Avon River, covering some 200 square miles with leafy greenery. Yet not far from the city a wealth of picturesque villages and historic houses nestle amid the undulating countryside. Between Birmingham and Coventry, an important city since the 14th century, and famed for its contro-

ENGLAND

versial cathedral that was designed by Sir Basil Spence and consecrated in 1962, as well as its mediaeval 'suffragette' Lady Godiva (the wife of Leofric, Earl of Mercia) who is reputed to have ridden naked through its streets in protest at the oppression of its inhabitants, stands the village of Meriden with its famous cross. Here too, is Packwood House with its remarkable 17th-century garden of shaped yew trees symbolising the Sermon on the Mount; Compton Wynyates, one of the most beautiful Tudor houses in England, and the site of the first major battle of the Civil War, in 1642; at high-ridged Edge Hill. South of Coventry the mediaeval fortress of Warwick Castle

dominates the wide-ribboned Avon as it flows gently through the pastoral landscape that has changed little since Warwickshire's famous bard inhabited the old market town of Stratford-upon-Avon. This famous birthplace of William Shakespeare, with its half-timbered black and white houses and red-brick Royal Shakespeare Theatre, has become one of the world's most famous tourist attractions, and from the poet's birthplace, the early-16th-century building in Henley Street, to his tomb in Holy Trinity Church, the fascination of the beautiful old town and its close affiliations with its son of genius can never fail to beguile and enrich each visitor.

Opposite page: The estuaries of the Lymington and Beaulieu Rivers are polka-dotted in summer with small craft bound for Lymington itself, with its Quay Hill below and Nelson Place left, or for Buckler's Hard above.

This page: Heavier shipping in the Solent tends to converge upon Southampton below and bottom, a vital transatlantic port.

Swan Green, Hampshire left is the perfect setting for a friendly game of cricket and an ideal starting point for outings in the New Forest.

ENGLAND

Drained to the Wash by the Welland and the Nene rivers, the fertile soil of the famous foxhunting county of Northamptonshire patterns the northern section of its agricultural landscape with a quilting of rich, arable fields. Its bustling county town on the Nene has long been noted for its shoe industry – confirmed by the fact that it was responsible for the supply of some 1,500 shoes for Cromwell's Roundheads during the Civil War. Charles II, however, was less than pleased with Northampton's compliance to fill the order, and wreaked his revenge in the destruction of its castle and town walls.

Like its neighbouring county, Leicestershire is primarily agricultural, with the emphasis on dairy farming: the delicious blue-veined Stilton cheese being produced near Melton Mowbray, the world-famous home of pork pies and the Quorn Hunt. It was here on the county's productive plains, at Bosworth Field, that the long-fought duels of the Wars of the Roses finally came to an end, when Henry of Lancaster was proclaimed Henry VII on the death of his adversary, the ill-fated Richard III, of the House of York. At the hub of the county town of Leicester,

Yarmouth top provides a colourful and popular harbour on the Isle of Wight. In recent years holiday-makers have also been drawn to the Channel Islands . . . to floodlit Mont Orgueil Castle above, to the sunset at La Corbière far left or to the imposing cliff scenery of Creux Harbor left. West of Eastbourne, the mainland coastline is dominated by chalk cliffs rising 600 feet above sea level at Beachy Head overleaf.

which boasts a modern university and a history dating back over 2,000 years, rises a Victorian, Gothic-inspired clock tower that pays tribute to four of the city's notable benefactors. The most famous of these was the powerful baron, Simon de Montfort, First Earl of Leicester, whose rebellion against the tyranny of his brother-in-law, Henry III, led to the establishment of the first English Parliament, in 1265. North-west of the city, beyond the once thickly-wooded slopes of Charnwood Forest, where, in ancient times, Bronze-Age men trod the craggy hills of Beacon Hill, stands Ashby-de-la-Zouch and its impressive ruined castle. Built in the 15th century by the First Lord Hastings, the castle was

Bodiam Castle left and top right is a magnificent fortress built in 1836 to drive French raiders from the River Rother. The Normans built the original Arundel Castle to defend the valley of the Arun River and its successor still dominates the valley right. Hastings with its charming Sinnock Square above has preserved much of its character and it was at Bosham overleaf that King Canute is said to have commanded the tide to roll back. Of more recent fame, Glyndebourne centre right has been known since 1934 for its music festivals.

ENGLAND

visited by many famous royal names, including Mary Queen of Scots, who twice stayed, as a most reluctant guest, in the custody of Lord Hasting's grandson, the First Earl of Huntingdon.

North Midlands

It is true that two centuries of industrial growth have inevitably left scars on the North Midlands horizon, yet to picture this area, which runs from the borders of Wales in the west to the North Sea-washed coastline in the east, as one vast, grimy, manufacturing community, would be quite erroneous. The five counties within its borders encompass an enormous diversity of scenery, from the scattered orchards of Salop, through the verdant woodlands of Sherwood Forest, to the notched stone crests of

Derbyshire's Peak District, whilst its roll-call of famous literary figures is firmly planted amid the ranks of those who have greatly contributed to the nation's cultural heritage.

South of the Severn River, the rich, sheep-farming country on the edge of the Clun Forest, dominated by the limestone ridge of Wenlock Edge, which was immortalised by A. E. Housman in 'A Shropshire Lad', is contrasted with the wild heathlands and wind-swept moors that mark the Welsh border, in Salop's fascinating south-west corner. Here stand the relics of fortified

strongholds that were built to defend against Celtic marauders – one of the most romantic being the abandoned, 11th-century sandstone castle of Ludlow, its crenellated towers perched high above the tranquil Teme River – as well as a wealth of well-preserved manor houses and clustered villages sporting their distinctive black and white, box-framed houses. North of the Long Mynd, a ten mile stretch of bleak hills that crest a vast acreage of heath

An onion-shaped dome and minarets adorn the Royal Pavilion, the Prince Regent's fantastic creation at Brighton left.

In 1834 the Duke of Devonshire inherited a small village on the south coast and set out to create from it a rival to the nearby town of Brighton. The result was Eastbourne far left, above and right top, centre and bottom, a watering place which was very popular in the 19th century and which has remained so to this day.

ENGLAND

and moorland that is peppered by pre-historic defence earthworks and barrows, sits beautiful Shrewsbury, the county town, idyllically situated in a loop of the Severn. The surrounding countryside is punctured by patches of hill country that includes the dramatic rock mass of the Wrekin, where a beacon once burned in warning of the coming of the Spanish Armada. During the 18th century Salop became the greatest iron-producing area in England; the town of Ironbridge, perched on the slopes of the steep and narrow gorge swept by the Severn River, gaining fame when Abraham Darby constructed the world's first cast-iron bridge, in 1779. Today the 200-ft bridge, cast in the designer's foundry at Coalbrookdale, is restricted to pedestrians.

Shoreham-by-Sea right is a harbour at the mouth of the River Adur, an idyllic haunt for small boat sailors.

Near Lewes the South Downs roll away in undulating countryside above left and on the downland turf above Wilmington appears the Long Man above. This tall figure, holding a staff in each of his outstretched hands, is believed to have been cut by the Saxons. Where the downs meet the sea between Beachy Head and the mouth of the Cuckmore River a dramatic cleft above right has earned the name of Birling Gap. Water lilies left cover one of the five lakes at Sheffield Park Gardens, whilst overleaf winter brings snow and ice to a house near Wisborough Green.

ENGLAND

Fine glazed china decorated with a spectrum of rainbow colours and gaily patterned earthenware; exquisitely moulded figurines and exotic vases; these are just some of the wares of 'The Potteries', the north Staffordshire region that has become famous throughout the world for its handsome artifacts and which is inextricably linked with the most noted porcelain and pottery manufacturing names of Wedgwood, Spode, Copeland and Minton. Centred around Stoke-on-Trent, the city was formed in the early part of the 20th century by the amalgamation of the five towns of Burslem, Hanley, Longton, Stoke and Tunstall, which featured prominently in the memorable novels of Arnold Bennett, and a sixth town, Fenton. It was over two centuries ago that Josiah Wedgwood brought lasting fame to the area, aided by the creative genius of his designer John Flaxman, although the industry is known to have existed long before the Roman occupation. Away from the busy areas of commerce, however, Staffordshire too has its great share of natural beauty, one of the most outstanding being glorious Cannock Chase, an oasis of heath and forest land that once formed a vast hunting ground for Plantagenet kings, which lies on the verge of south Staffordshire's Black Country.

Derbyshire's Peak District, with its lush valleys and cascading streams, winding rivers and tree-studded hills, great rocky crags and gentle undulating pastures, has been compared to the countryside of Switzerland, and has a scenic splendour that would be difficult to surpass anywhere in the world. It came as no surprise, therefore, when in 1951 over five hundred square miles of the county were designated an area of outstanding beauty and became Britain's first

Rye right was once a hill fort ringed by the sea. The waters receded in the late-16th century but the town has never lost the individuality of its cobbled streets above.

Facing page: Lovely old houses bottom left and the renowned Mermaid Inn top left, which opened its doors in 1420, recall the days when Rye was a vital port. East Grinstead centre left has preserved its market town atmosphere and in Brighton, the Lanes far right survive from the original fishing hamlet. At Chilham overleaf Tudor houses surround the picturesque village square.

ENGLAND

National Park. As might be expected in such a lovely setting, great country houses were built here by famous families. South of the town of Bakewell, famed as the home of the delicious Bakewell tarts, lies the turreted, mediaeval outline of Haddon Hall, a romantic old house surrounded by terraced gardens. Not far away, and in contrast to its almost rambling beauty, stands one of the truly great stately homes of England, the majestic classical mansion of Chatsworth House, set amid exquisite landscaped grounds, and built for the first Duke of Devonshire in the early 18th century.

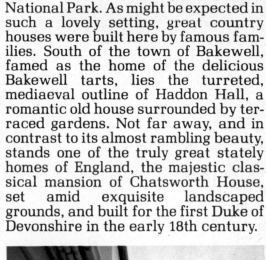

While part of Nottinghamshire's face undeniably reveals the scars of industrialisation, notably in the collieries and their attendant slag heaps across the north-west coalfield belt, so vividly portrayed in the works of D. H. Lawrence, its boundaries encompass not only the 200,000 acres of flat agricultural land of the Isle of Axholme which was drained by the Dutchman, Cornelius Vermuyden in the 17th century, but also the green woodlands of romantic Sherwood Forest, the home of England's most popular folk hero, the elusive Robin Hood. It is true that the famous outlaw is identified with no less than ten other counties in the

ENGLAND

country and that Barnsdale Forest in Yorkshire has an equal claim to be called his home, yet somehow the remnants of the once-vast Sherwood Forest seem richer in association with the man whom tradition asserts is more fact than fiction.

The ferry from Hull in Humberside makes its way across the River Humber to New Holland in Lincolnshire. The area has more in common with the low-lying country of Holland than just a name, for it too is just about at sea level, and in springtime the fields are alive with the colours of the tulips that are grown in the rich soil of this part of the country. Yet not all the lands of Lincolnshire are flat and low-lying, by any means. There are also the rolling uplands of the Wolds, thick with sheep grazing on the pastures, and abundant in the wheat for which the area is so famous. In this countryside of hills and valleys may be found many charming villages and towns, including the birthplace of Alfred, Lord Tennyson, in Somersby. Of the county's many churches, abbeys, stately homes and other fine buildings, two stand out in

Kent is strewn with villages, where time seems almost to have passed unnoticed. Among the most attractive are Chartwell above; Farningham with its weather-boarded mill centre right and Chilham, which still boasts a very fine 15th-century inn top right.

This county is also rich in buildings of historical interest. Knole right, one of the largest and most celebrated homes in England, dates from 1465 and served as palace for a succession of Archbishops of Canterbury.

particular, though for different reasons. The first is in the ancient town of Boston, on the River Witham and is known by the peculiar name of 'The Boston Stump'. It is, in fact, the tower of St Botolph's Church and is a landmark for many miles. The second is, not surprisingly, the magnificent cathedral that dominates the city of Lincoln which contains, in the Angel Choir, the finest decorated work to be found in the country.

The North West

Ranged along the convoluted coastline that overlooks the Irish Sea, with its back against the spiny Pennine Mountain Chain, the North West counties present not only a rich diversity of landscape that encompasses the celebrated Lakeland scenery of Cumbria, and the park-like countryside of the Cheshire Plain, but also a striking difference in character and accent

Hever Castle above is a moated, 13th-century manor house in which Anne Boleyn spent her girlhood, and Scotney Castle right was originally a Tudor manor. Most famous of all these buildings, Canterbury Cathedral overleaf, which dates from Norman times, still stands resplendent as the Mother Church of Anglicans throughout the world.

ENGLAND

that has persisted throughout the centuries.

Grassy banks of yellow-headed buttercups; wooded hilltops bearing traces of long-ago Roman occupation; gentle rivers curving through fertile farmland; picturesque towns with their distinctive 'magpie' houses, and timbered manors, beautifully illustrated in the 15th-century building of Bramall Hall and 16th-century Little Moreton Hall, are part of the immense, individual charm of Cheshire. It was at Knutsford that Mrs. Gaskell drew inspiration for her charming novel, 'Cranford', although the sight of the giant radio telescope of Jodrell Bank, standing like some science fiction creation, six miles south of the town, would doubtfully have gained the approbation of her 'genteel' ladies, to whom artificial satellites, radio signals and far-distant galaxies would have been an undreamed-of horror! Chester, the county town, skirted by the meandering River Dee, is an ancient walled city of Roman origin, with

In Royal Tunbridge Wells left and above, the Pantiles, an 18th-century shopping walk shaded by lime trees, has changed little since the town was in its prime as an elegant Regency spa. The tranquillity of former years still prevails beneath the pillars of its gracious buildings.

a wealth of historic interest. Probably its most famous feature is The Rows, which consists of galleried streets of shops, reached by stairways; a feature that is quite unique. There is also what is believed to be the last surviving example of a sedan-chair, at the odd-sounding address of No. 13 City Walls. Cheshire, too, however, also has its own industrial areas, particularly those connected with the textile industry, as well as a salt mine at Winsford – proof that not all of this valuable mineral is of Siberian extraction.

Between the estuaries of the Rivers Mersey and Dee lies the Wirral Peninsula, the heart of the Merseyside playground, where miles of sand-dune-edged beaches are connected to the industrialised hub of Birkenhead by wharves and docks. Conjoined to this important flour-milling and ship-building centre by two tunnels under the Mersey, is the 13th-century fishing village that grew phenomenally during the Industrial Revolution – Liverpool – Europe's greatest Atlantic seaport. From the seven-mile stretch of densely-packed dockland along its waterfront

Weatherboarded houses line the streets of Tenterden above, the birthplace of William Caxton, the father of English printing, while Tudor and Jacobean houses are the hallmark of Chilham centre right. In Canterbury, beautiful half-timbered cottages overlook the West Gate gardens top right.

In a setting ablaze with flowers, the charming old building in Headcorn right has become almost a symbol of the county in which it has stood for so many years.

ENGLAND

rises the idiosyncratic outline of the celebrated Liver Building, its two main towers topped by mythical 'Liver' birds, after which the city is said to have been named. This cosmopolitan city also boasts two cathedrals, each of distinct, ecclesiastical architecture: Sir Giles Gilbert Scott's Gothic-inspired Anglican Cathedral and Sir Frederick Gibberd's contemporary Roman Catholic Metropolitan Cathedral, with its huge, conical 'lantern'.

Until the re-organisation of the county boundaries in 1974, Manchester, built by Agricola's legions on the banks of the Irwell River, was the mighty commercial hub of Lancashire, a 14th-century county palatine, bordered by the wild Pennine Moors on its eastern flank and by fertile lowlands to the west, against the Irish Sea. It is along this coastline, a popular resort area since the mid-18th century, that is

At Cranbrook above, a splendid octagonal windmill, built in the early-19th century, has been carefully restored and is still operative, and not far from Tonbridge, the traditional Kent oast houses right have been carefully converted into homes. More conventional in style, the church at Ightham far right is nevertheless a characteristic part of the county's charm. Aylesford above far right is a pretty village on the Medway, famous for its restored Carmelite friary.

ENGLAND

sited the North West's busiest and most famous holiday centre of Blackpool, dominated by its 518 ft tower that oversees the six-mile long promenade, noted for its spectacular autumn illuminations. Off-shore lies one of the smallest independent sovereign countries under the crown, the tiny Isle of Man, its picturesque scenery and exceptionally mild climate providing ideal conditions for holiday activities. Douglas, the island's capital, is the home of the Tynwald, the Manx Parliament of Scandinavian origins that are earlier than those of Westminster.

Harnessed to the vast conurbation of Greater Manchester, and its fan of industrial centres that include the major cotton-spinning towns of Bolton and Oldham, Manchester's importance as a key cotton centre was firmly rooted during the 18th century, although Flemish weavers had established the weaving tradition over four hundred years earlier. This inland city became one of the country's largest seaports, handling the export of raw cotton and importing finished textiles, with the construction of the 35½-mile-long Manchester Ship Canal, which was opened in 1894. Although ravaged by the effects of the Industrial Revolution and by bomb damage during the Second World War, the city's extensive redevelopment schemes have already greatly altered and enhanced its visual image, but its crowning glory, however, is still the magnificent 15th-

Wooded hills sweep across parts of Surrey, and cottages such as that shown right remain unspoilt by their proximity to London. The old wool town of Godalming below has streets and buildings of Tudor and Stuart days and Dorking's High Street bottom right boasts the White Horse Inn, where once Charles Dickens stayed. In Guildford Sir Edward Maufe's new cathedral dominates Stag Hill bottom but the old Guildhall left still bears a clock made in 1683. The Royal Coat of Arms far left presides over an entrance gate to Kew Gardens. Crowds throng the Epsom Downs overleaf for the famous Derby.

ENGLAND

century Perpendicular Gothic Cathedral, its soaring, 280 ft tower containing a carillon of 23 bells.

Lake-strewn valleys amid craggy mountains, fern-covered hillsides and forested woodlands, tumbling waterfalls and carpets of wild flowers; little wonder that the spectacular scenery of Cumbria's Lake District inspired the celebrated 'Lake Poets' – Wordsworth, Southey and Coleridge – and a host of writers such as Beatrix Potter, who wrote and illustrated some of her charming children's books at Hill Top Farm in the village of Sawrey. Painters and photographers, sportsmen and

ramblers, and, of course, mountaineers, who challenge the forbidding massifs that include Skiddaw, Helvellyn and England's second highest peak, Scafell, have also long been attracted to the Lakeland region, where, it is claimed, the sport of rock-climbing originated. The two largest lakes, Ullswater and Windermere are set amid a landscape that has remained virtually unchanged since Wordsworth first saw his 'host of golden daffodils', while the Tarns, near Coniston, is considered by many to be the prettiest of all the area's lakes. Yet Cumbria does not consist solely of Lakeland, as un-

questionable as its beauty is. The Border region beyond Carlisle is rich in historical associations and remains. Here stand the fragments of the northern limit of the Roman Empire – Hadrian's Wall – and a wealth of prehistoric sites and castles, like the Border fortress of Carlisle Castle. Notable industrial centres include those of Whitehaven and Workington, while the Cumbrian coast, site of the Calder Hall atomic power station, reveals long stretches of sandy beaches, that, coupled with beautiful inland countryside, remain quite unspoiled for the enjoyment of all.

North East England

Once a part of the vast Anglo-Saxon kingdom of Northumbria, ruled at its inception by Aethelfrith during the early 7th century, the North East counties have been bound not only by their associated historical links but also by their common, natural resources of coal and iron-ore that contributed significantly to the industrial development initiated during the 18th century. Their rugged landscapes, too, from the wild, wind-blown Pennine Moors stretching northwards towards the Cheviot

ENGLAND

Hills, to their river-drained valleys, have much in common. Its history is possibly the most turbulent of England's regions, and it was not until after the Acts of Union – legislation uniting the Crowns of England and Scotland – in 1707, that the region began to develop its true potential. The boundaries of the three original counties of Yorkshire, Durham and Northumberland were effectively reorganised in 1974 and now comprise the above-listed seven counties; yet governmental demarcation lines cannot blot out their inextricable ties,

From Kew Bridge a footpath leads to the Thames north-bank area of Strand-on-the-Green above, a secluded spot where most of the houses are still Georgian. Inside the Royal Botanic Gardens at Kew, a Chinese pagoda facing page, left, designed by Sir William Chambers, has provoked much curiosity since its construction in 1761.

Traditionally the pond on the village green plays a vital role in English country life. At Chiddingford facing page, right, a lily-covered pool serves as a mirror for the parish church, and at Outwood left ducks remain determinedly on familiar waters, undeterred by winter frost and ice.

St George's Chapel, Windsor overleaf is possibly the finest example of Perpendicular architecture in England.

ENGLAND

forged by a shared experience throughout eons of time.

Centred around the Humber Estuary, the county of Humberside comprises most of the old East Riding of Yorkshire, plus the area around Goole. It was along the chalk-cliffed coastline where the Yorkshire Wolds terminate in the rocky promontory of Flamborough Head, just beyond the popular sea-side resort of Bridlington, that the Vikings successfully swept ashore in the 10th century – their once-victorious cries now echoed by the high-pitched shrieks of thousands of seabirds which today inhabit the striking northern cliffs. Officially Kingston-upon-Hull, Hull, lying on the broad Humber River and one of the country's leading seaports, is renowned for its great fishing fleets which have justly earned their reputation of landing a greater quantity of fish than any other British port. The city is also remembered as the native town of the dedicated anti-slavery campaigner William Wilber-

force, whose home is now a museum. Of the county's many fascinating towns and villages, however, the most splendid is undoubtedly Beverley, with its glorious, twin-towered Gothic Minster, a flourishing market town since the Middle Ages, and the birthplace of the late-mediaeval martyr Bishop John Fisher.

Windsor Castle, in Berkshire these pages, is a favourite home of the Royal Family and the largest castle in England, covering 13 acres. Founded by William the Conqueror, it first became a royal residence in the reign of Queen Victoria. The castle itself has been altered considerably in the course of history but it is still the scene of colourful pageantry and processions such as that of the Garter Ceremony right and overleaf, attended by Her Majesty the Queen and watched by huge and enthusiastic crowds.

ENGLAND

Formed mainly from the former North Riding, the diverse landscape of North Yorkshire, littered with the remains of man from time immemorial, encompasses the wild, bleak North York Moors that rise beyond the Vale of Pickering, bordering the Yorkshire Wolds, and the broad expanse of the fertile Vale of York which is flanked to the west by the spectacular scenery of the Yorkshire Dales as they merge with England's spiny backbone, the Pennine Chain. In a region crammed with so many historical relics, it is difficult to do other than just pluck at random some of its bright jewels: close to Malton stands one of England's most palatial mansions in a perfectly matched setting, that of Castle Howard, created for the 3rd Earl of Carlisle by Sir John Vanbrugh, between 1699 and 1726; by the Wharfe River tower the splendid ruined remains of twelfth-century Bolton Abbey, and near Helmsley, above the River Rye, is sited one of the country's earliest Cistercian houses, magnificent Rievaulx Abbey, its ruined splendour seen to perfection against a densely-wooded backdrop. Popular sea-side resorts, such as Scarborough and Whitby, dot its coastline; dignified towns, like the fashionable inland spa of Harrogate, which is also a noted conference centre, add to its lustre, whilst a host of picturesque villages are scattered across its length and breadth. As if this were not enough, proud Yorkshiremen can also boast of their ancient Roman garrison-town of Eboracum – glorious York – much of its 2,000 years of history still vividly tangible inside the city walls. Its present name is derived from Jorvik, so called by the invading Danes who captured the city during the 9th century. Of all its treasures, however, pride of place must go to its breath-taking Minster, 'a poem of stone' that took over two and a half centuries to complete, between 1220 and 1470.

Famed for its woollen industry, centred on the important trading communities that include Bradford, Leeds and Halifax, which grew phenomenally during the Industrial Revolution as the old cottage industries moved closer to the coalfields and their valuable source of fuel, the West Yorkshire Moors, penetrated by the Aire and Calder rivers, have long supported the white-fleeced sheep that have grazed on the moorland for centuries past. It was this same bleak moorland turf that was trod by the famous Brontë family – Emily, Charlotte, Anne and Branwell, who lived in the romantic Old Parsonage at Haworth, a square, sandstone house that has been the Brontë Museum since 1928.

Below the moors the industrial heart of Yorkshire is contained within the metropolitan county of South Yorkshire. This largely industrialised region, especially in the Don Valley, is renowned for its iron and steel manufacture. Sheffield, set in an amphitheatre of the South Pennine slopes, is

Although inevitably dominated by its magnificent castle and by the colour of Royal pomp, the largely Victorian town of Windsor on these pages is itself very attractive.

The portrait of Her Majesty the Queen bottom left was painted by Pietro Annigoni in 1954 and the painting bottom, was executed by Sir William Hutchison for the Auckland Savings Bank, New Zealand.

synonymous with the steel and cutlery industry, for the city has produced knife blades here for almost seven centuries.

Rugged and tempered like the stalwart people who laid not only their endeavour but also their landscape at the feet of progress during the Industrial Revolution, the counties of Cleveland, Durham and Tyne & Wear still bear, inevitably, the symbols that mark the region's industrial greatness. Yet it would be erroneous to suppose that the counties consist solely of the features of ship-building, iron, steel and chemical industries, for they too have their share of beauty, and nowhere is this more apparent than in the splendid cathedral city of Durham, built round a loop in the River Wear; its magnificent Norman Cathedral a shrine of St Cuthbert and also containing the tomb of the Venerable Bede within its richly ornamented interior. Along the coastline picturesque resorts boast long stretches of sandy beaches, while some of the finest scenery of the Pennine Chain is evident on the west Durham Moors.

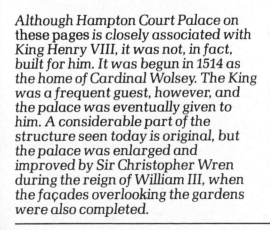

Although Hampton Court Palace on these pages is closely associated with King Henry VIII, it was not, in fact, built for him. It was begun in 1514 as the home of Cardinal Wolsey. The King was a frequent guest, however, and the palace was eventually given to him. A considerable part of the structure seen today is original, but the palace was enlarged and improved by Sir Christopher Wren during the reign of William III, when the façades overlooking the gardens were also completed.

ENGLAND

Rich in history, England's most northerly county of Northumberland, bounded on the north by Scotland across the River Tweed and the Cheviot Hills, and flanked to the east by the North Sea, contains one of the most famous of all Roman remains – the spectacular relic of Hadrian's Wall which slices across the county from Haltwhistle to Wallsend in Tyne & Wear. Today, the tranquil farmland, south of the River Tweed, belies the savagery of the fierce Border Clashes – vividly evoked by the area's many ancient fortresses – perhaps the bloodiest that of Flodden Field where, in 1513, the blood of James IV and thousands of Scots and Englishmen

was spilled on the earth now covered by tall ears of corn that flutter gently in the breeze. At Berwick-upon-Tweed, England's northernmost town, which was once a great Scottish port, stands an impressive stone bridge, of 17th-century origin, with no less than 15 arches; built by order of James I to connect the town of Tweedmouth on the opposite side of the estuary.

England is a country with a rich and varied past, whose kings, queens and nobles have left it liberally endowed with a vast store of fortresses, castles and palaces that can be seen throughout its length and breadth. Among its greatest glories, however, are a wealth of religious establishments – monasteries, abbeys, cathedrals and the like – many of which were partly or totally destroyed during various upheavals, particularly during the Dissolution and the Civil War. Nevertheless, a magnificent collection of ecclesiastical treasures in stone still remain and are considered to be amongst the finest in Europe.

The quiet scenes of English country life, the inspiration of so many artists and writers, have remained a reality in many parts of the country: left Marlow in Buckinghamshire, above the old mill at Hambledon, above left a snow-covered country churchyard and far right 'Ye Old Bell' public house in Hurley.

Henley-on-Thames was the scene of the world's first regatta in 1839 and the Henley Royal Regatta right has remained one of the great national institutions, held annually in July.

In Blenheim Park, near Woodstock, stands Blenheim Palace above right, the celebrated birthplace of Sir Winston Churchill. The grandiose masterpiece of Sir John Vanbrugh, it was originally built for John Churchill, the first Duke of Marlborough.

ENGLAND

England's Ecclesiastical and Architectural Glories.

Canterbury Cathedral.

Exeter Cathedral.

Gloucester Cathedral.

Ely Cathedral.

Durham Cathedral.

*'Come, thou holy Paraclete,
and from thy celestial seat send
thy light and brilliancy.'*

The words of the thirteenth-century Archbishop, Stephen Langton, summarise the intent of mediaeval architecture to create on earth a reflection of God's heaven. The age is often looked upon as a harsh, unremitting period which seemingly awaited the Renaissance to liberate it from the confines of unquestioning belief. However, such a viewpoint belies the greatest of treasures – the incredibly rich, diverse and splendid cathedral churches which adorn our land.

These highlights of national heritage are prayers in stone raised on high by the sons of God – who drew their strength and resolve from implicit faith – to the eternal glory of their Father above. Thus, by their very nature, Romanesque and Gothic cathedrals speak to the soul alone – in carving, in glass and in the very shape and construction of the building. No other age could have furnished so great a majesty, confidently expressing the belief that the glory due to the Lord should not be tarnished by the squalor of His house. Clearly it is impossible to encapsulate the whole field of their art; yet the cathedrals represent that unique pinnacle to which the spirit may be uplifted.

Viewed from Christchurch Meadows right, the tower of Merton College rises to join the many 'dreaming spires', for which Oxford is renowned.

ENGLAND

Canterbury Cathedral

Canterbury has been the very heart of Christian worship in England since Whitsuntide AD 597 when St Augustine baptised Ethelbert, the Jutish King of Kent. The cathedral that grew from his mission is as rich and as grand in architecture and history as befits the mother church of the Anglican faith, the See of the Primate of All England, and the focal point of the cult of St Thomas à Becket – the Archbishop who was slain in the shadows of his own cathedral church. Four years after the martyrdom, as if to purify the dreadful sacrilege, flame swept through the old building to reduce the Norman work to a charred ruin. Afforded the opportunity to develop, in a practical shape, the passion that filled the universal heart of England, the cathedral we know

The Bodleian Library above is one of the oldest and most important non-lending reference libraries in the world and the nearby Radcliffe Camera above far right serves as one of the university reading rooms. More formidable in their associations, the Examination Schools, part of which may be seen centre right are the setting for all university examinations. The quadrangles above right and right are those of St Edmund Hall and Nuffield College and the façade far right is part of St John's College.

ENGLAND

today was raised to Becket, 'in admiration of his self-sacrifice, in veneration of his piety, and in yearning to do him honour'. These were the moving powers which erected anew the long-drawn aisles of nave and choir; to turn the scene of his Passion into a building which is Thomas à Becket's enduring monument – a building whose geometry of strength and sinew was lovingly described as a 'door open unto Heaven'.

The pre-eminence of Canterbury, however, extends far beyond the time of the martyr to the missionary Augustine, who, with forty monks, was sent by Pope Gregory to effect the conversion of England. He landed at Ebbsfleet in Thanet and made the short journey across Kent to preach before King Ethelbert at Canterbury. Although the King's wife, Bertha, was already a Christian, Ethelbert was suspicious of the new faith and only consented to listen to Augustine's preaching seated underneath an oak tree – beneath whose sacred branches he need fear neither spells nor incantations placed upon him – yet such was the persuasion of the apostle's message that Ethelbert and most of his household were baptised in the faith.

A simple oblong church, with an apse at the east end, stood upon the cathedral site and was dedicated to 'Christ our Saviour' but, within sixty years of Augustine's death, plague so dramatically swept the Saxon kingdoms that many returned to the heathenism of their past. The man who re-established order was Archbishop Theodore of Tarsus, a member of the Eastern Church who, despite his sixty-six years, possessed great energy of the spirit and spent much of his episcopate travelling the countryside, reconciling men once more to the Christian faith. The Venerable Bede says of him, 'he was the first Archbishop that all the English consented to obey' – a position of supremacy enjoyed by his successors ever since. Indeed, such was the power and influence of the office that, in Norman times, appointment to it was the prerogative of the Crown. Thus, King William I replaced the Saxon Stigand with his own nominee – the seventy year old Lanfranc, late Abbot of Caen. He rebuilt the destroyed Saxon church, flanking the building with twin towers, each with pinnacles of gold; whilst at its centre a

golden angel surmounted the crossing tower. Hardly was the church finished than Lanfranc's successor, Anselm, pulled down the new choir and extended eastwards, adding another pair of transepts and doubling the length of the previous building. A twelfth-century fresco has recently come to light in St Anselm's Chapel. It owes its excellent state of preservation to a buttress which had covered the painting since the early years of the Middle Ages. The theme is 'St Paul

Established in 1214, the University of Oxford is the second oldest in Europe. The collegiate system began in the late-13th century with the founding of four colleges, among them University College right. Christ Church above was founded by Cardinal Wolsey in 1525. Its college chapel, originally the Church of St Frideswide, is the cathedral of the diocese.

and the Viper' – an incident from his mission which has rarely been represented in art – 'And when Paul had gathered a bundle of sticks, and laid them on the fire, there came a viper out of the heat, and fastened on his hand. And when the barbarians saw the venomous beast hang on his hand, they said among themselves, No doubt this man is a murderer, whom, though he hath escaped the sea, yet vengeance suffereth not to live. And he shook off the beast into the fire, and felt no harm. Howbeit . . . they changed their minds, and said that he was a god'.

The crypt, a rare survivor of Anselm's cathedral, is the largest Norman crypt in the world. It was built

Oxford's 'Bridge of Sighs' above left forms a particularly attractive part of Hertford College.

Magdalen College above, founded by William of Waynflete in 1458, is one of the largest and most beautiful of all the colleges. Its most imposing feature is the Perpendicular bell-tower, begun in 1492 and completed in 1509. Here the choristers sing their Latin hymn at five o'clock on May-day morning.

by Prior Ernulf and includes a quite remarkable collection of lively and imaginative carvings which are wrought into the stone capitals of the undercroft's short, sturdy piers. They are primarily secular in nature; some of the subjects are taken from fables such as Reynard the Fox, whilst others rely purely upon the imagination of their creator, for example, a hybrid ram-woman plays a fiddle accompanied on the pipes by a goat who wrestles with a dragon. The style is close to the contemporary illuminations in the Canterbury Scriptorium. It was subjects such as these which were soon to be denounced by St Bernard as 'unclean apes, fierce lions, monstrous centaurs and half men'. The powerful groined vault which the columns support is derived directly from the barrel-vaults of Roman architecture and indicates the close affinity

Punting on the River Isis top is a traditional summer recreation. The Romans called the Thames at Oxford the Isis. Exactly where the Thames becomes the Isis and vice versa is not clearly defined but the river flows undeterred through this great seat of learning just as it flows through Goring lock left and right, Wallingford lock above and Whitchurch above right. At Henley above left it makes another claim to fame as the setting for the celebrated regatta.

between the English Romanesque (Norman) and its classical predecessor. In the northern transept of the crypt are the ancient chapels of St Mary Magdelene, St Nicholas and St Gabriel. On the apse vault of the latter chapel is a Byzantine fresco depicting Gabriel's annunciation to Zacharias and to Mary; and the subsequent birth of John the Baptist and the Saviour Jesus. The crypt's main feature is the 'Chapel of Our Lady of the Undercroft', a gift financed by the Black Prince – the price he had to pay for a papal dispensation to marry his cousin Joan, the

ENGLAND

'Fair Maid of Kent'. Behind the forest of arches which surround the altar lay for fifty years the body of St Thomas.

Even before Becket's death prompted Canterbury to become one of the premier shrines of Europe the old Norman cathedral could justifiably claim to be the holiest place in England. Its relics attracted the forefathers of Chaucer's pilgrims to the bodies of twelve saints interred within. In particular, the shrines of St Anselm, St Odo, St Dunstan and St Alphege proved popular – the inclusion of the latter caused heated debate among those who considered him unworthy of veneration, for he had been struck down during a drunken brawl, and pelted to death with ox bones by Norsemen. The cathedral also possessed the supposed arm of St George 'still with dry blood and the flesh upon it'.

In 1170, to dominate all, came the martyrdom of Archbishop Thomas à Becket, who perished within Lanfranc's Romanesque cathedral. Four years later cinders and sparks carried by the wind settled upon the church roof, caught between the joists, and sent showers of molten lead into Prior

Suffolk villages such as Sapiston below and Cavendish bottom left have been the inspiration of many, but Suffolk is above all Constable country. John Constable was born in the county in 1776 and went to school at Lavenham right, one of the most resplendent of Suffolk wool towns with fine mediaeval timber houses. The original Wool Hall has been incorporated into the popular Swan Hotel below left.

Conrad's 'glorious choir': much of the building that Becket had known and loved went up in gusts of flame. After recovering from their shock, the brethren consulted how best to repair the damage. French and English 'artificers' were summoned, among whom was William of Sens, 'a man active and ready as a workman most skilled both in wood and stone, to him and the providence of God, was the execution of the work committed'.

It was a master-stroke that saw William of Sens' new architectural vision rise from the ashes of the old, a noble edifice soaring ever-upwards to its climax in triumphant symbolism of the martyr's apotheosis. Canterbury cathedral received tithes from the lands it owned and was, by the standards of the day, a rich establishment; obligations offered to their new saint proved a source of ever-loosened purse strings expressed by a building programme designed to reflect the devotion that Becket inspired. Thus the cathedral owes its present splendour to the gifts of those who came to honour his mediaeval shrine.

ENGLAND

It is to William of Sens, the builder of Canterbury's choir, 1175-1180, that we owe the introduction of the new Gothic style into England. Its use of the pointed arch, to replace the Romanesque semi-circular arch, makes the style an architecture of line rather than volume – of forces held in equilibrium rather than weight supported by mass. The feeling is to be experienced in his choir, where its essentially linear character is emphasised by the slender shafts of Purbeck marble and the ribs of the sexpartite vault: the novelty was clear – even at that time. Such was

Walsham le Willows left is set in the heart of tree-studded parkland and Clacton-on-Sea below is a busy Victorian-Edwardian seaside town with all the accompanying attractions.

ENGLAND

Canterbury's prestige throughout England that others followed the distinctive style of the Gothic. In 1178 William of Sens fell 50 ft. from the scaffolding of the choir and was gravely injured. The task of continuing his work was entrusted to a younger colleague, William the Englishman, 'small of body, but in workmanship of many kinds acute and honest'. By 1180 he had sufficiently finished the choir for the monks to start using the high

Finchingfield above left; Sisted, with its snow-covered churchyard left, and Kersey above, are the epitome of the English village. Willy Lott's Cottage at Flatford, one of John Constable's most celebrated subjects, is shown overleaf, and top Lavenham's Tudor Guildhall.

ENGLAND

Burghley House left, begun in 1552 by Sir William Cecil, is one of England's greatest Elizabethan houses.

Norfolk is perhaps best known for its Broads below and below left which offer 200 miles of navigable water. Yet, despite the influx of boating enthusiasts, the county has preserved its past in the graceful windmills which preside even over the quay at Cley-next-the-Sea right.

altar for services. During the next twenty years William progressed to the transepts, the ambulatory and the corona. His most important task, however, was the erection of the Trinity Chapel – the site chosen to house the remains of the now canonised Becket. By raising the Trinity above the level of the choir he achieved a feeling of triumphant ascension, evoked by successive flights of steps that led pilgrims up from the level of the nave, and conducted them through the exceptionally long 200 ft. length of choir, chancel and Trinity Chapel, into the presence of the shrine: as one palmer commented, 'church seems to be piled upon church, a new temple entered as soon as the first is ended'.

The jubilee of his martyrdom in 1220 saw Becket's body transferred in great state from the undercroft to the 'glorious summit' of William the Englishman's Trinity Chapel. In the

ENGLAND

centuries that followed he received the devotion of all the nations of Christendom. It was to his shrine at Canterbury that the Emperor Emmanuel of Byzantine and Sigismund the Emperor of the West paid homage; as did King Henry VIII and the Emperor Charles IV, who knelt side by side at his tomb. Here also King Edward I gave the golden crown of conquered Scotland, and King Louis VII offered up the famous jewel, the 'Régale de France' (said to be worth a 'King's ransom') for the safe deliverance of his son from illness. The pageant of the shrine is marvellously captured in the 'miracle windows' of the Trinity Chapel and the corona, which reflect the wealth of incident that occurred around Becket's tomb. The stained glass ranks amongst the finest in the world and must have excited almost as great a wonder as the shrine itself.

Archbishop Sudbury ordered work to begin on a new nave in 1379 (the former nave of Lanfranc had survived the fire but was falling into decay). He engaged Henry Yevele, the greatest English architect of the Middle Ages. As King's Master Mason since 1360, it was he who was responsible for diffusing the Perpendicular style throughout the realm, thus creating a national art. As Yevele had done earlier at Gloucester Cathedral, he created a masterpiece at Canterbury – built when the Becket cult had raised the cathedral to the heights of its worldly glory.

The close of the fifteenth century saw the mediaeval 'Angle Steeple' replaced by John Westall's 'Bell Harry Tower', the strong vertical lines and shallow mouldings of which emphasise the upward thrust of the tower's 235

ft. It is named after the great bell, 'Harry', a gift of Prior Henry of Eastry, and is one of the glories of the Perpendicular style – long esteemed as the 'chastest and most beautiful specimen we possess of pointed architecture'. Its height counterbalances the vast length of the cathedral, which was raised on high to assert its spiritual authority over miles of surrounding Kentish countryside, beckoning pilgrims to worship at the martyr's side. His tomb, however, was despoiled in 1538, St Thomas' body was burnt

Horning left on the River Bure between Wroxham and Acle is a very popular angling and sailing centre and Sheringham below left is a busy fishing port and resort, but Norfolk has much to offer apart from its coast and waterways. Pictured above are the ruins of Castle Acre and below a fascinating model village at Great Yarmouth.

and his ashes were scattered to the four winds. The shrine and all its contents disappeared; but a more touching reminder of his greatness remains – the hollowed depressions in the hard stone of step and pavement, worn away by the knees of countless numbers of worshippers who flocked to his shrine from every Christian land.

Potter Heigham left provides attractive moorings for yachts on the Norfolk Broads.

Norwich, once a centre of the wool trade, is a city full of fascinating old buildings such as those in Tombeland Alley below. Beyond them rises the distinctive spire of the city's mainly Norman cathedral.

ENGLAND

Exeter Cathedral

Exeter Cathedral, the realm's finest example of the Decorated style, echoes to a 'mysterious ringing of song', seemingly frozen within its stonework. The effect is evoked by one of England's architectural glories – the cathedral nave and choir, which comprise the largest uninterrupted stretch of Gothic vaulting in the world. Their harmony and balance produce in the spectator that particular and miraculous 'singing of the mind' which only the greatest of architectural effects may achieve. It embodies the sense once described by the German Romantic. Schlegel, in that the purest

The University of Cambridge was established early in the 13th century and, as at Oxford, its development was marked by the foundation of colleges which stand nobly in a setting of river and gardens. Trinity College overleaf with its Nevile's Court right was founded initially in 1336 by Edward III, then refounded by Henry VIII in 1546. Clare College above, far right, originally University Hall, was founded in 1320 and Emmanuel above right was instituted in 1584.

The lovely bridge of Trinity College spans the River Cam above while the Cambridge 'Bridge of Sighs' far right links two of the buildings of St John's College. Yet Cambridge does not hold a monopoly on the county's fine architecture. Ely Cathedral above, centre right, begun in 1083, is a magnificent sight, even from a distance.

ENGLAND

forms of mediaeval architecture are in themselves 'frozen music'.

The founding of Exeter cathedral can be traced to the year 1049, when its first bishop, Leofric, was granted royal permission to transfer the government of his diocese from the defenceless village of Crediton down river to the walled city of Exeter. He also founded the cathedral library, bequeathing a collection of manuscripts, among which is the famous Exeter Book, the largest single source of Anglo-Saxon verse. It was written between AD 950 – 985 and includes 'The Wanderer', a poem reflecting the sorrows of banishment, 'Oft a solitary mortal wishes for grace, his Maker's mercy. Though sick at heart he must long traverse the watery ways, with his hands must stir the rime-cold sea, and tread the paths of exile.'

The suppression of the neighbouring

Punts make their way along the River Cam right past an abundance of fine architecture. St John's College overleaf was founded by the mother of Henry VII in the 16th century. Possibly the greatest glory of Cambridge, however, is King's College Chapel above right, one of the finest Gothic buildings in Europe.

The graves in the American Cemetery in Cambridgeshire above are those of American servicemen who lost their lives in combat during the Second World War. The view left shows the striking interior of the cemetery's Memorial.

ENGLAND

Cornish See of St Germans increased the power of the Bishopric of Exeter and, with lucrative tithes from the flourishing Cornish tin mines, the bishop received substantial revenues which, through personal munificence, were channelled toward the greater glory of God. Thus commenced in 1275 a century of improvements and re-building, on a scale in keeping with the See's increasing influence, which culminated in the creation of the cathedral as we know it today.

The challenge of transforming the Norman church (with its distinctive twin towers) was chiefly inspired by Bishop Walter Branscombe, who built the rectochoir and Lady Chapel. His successor, Bishop Peter Quivil, directed much of his wealth towards converting the original towers of 1107 into transepts – a job which involved building the huge Decorated windows and cutting splendid arches into the

Norman fabric. Thereafter each bishop added his own distinctive improvement.

John Grandisson received the bish-opric in 1327 and during his forty-two year reign was to realise the success-ful conclusion of the long and difficult work begun by Branscombe. The con-struction of the nave was entrusted to Thomas Witney and the vaulted roof was executed by Richard Farleigh, the architect of Salisbury's spire. Despite the long and often arduous progress of its building (1328-1369), the nave remains faithful to the main elements of the earlier work at the cathedral's east end. The glorious 'palm vaulting'

with its multiple tiercerons extends (unbroken by a central tower) along the entire length of nave and choir. This vault – the most poetic in England – together with the exuberant stone carvings and elaborate window traceries combine at Exeter to present English Decorated Gothic at its very best. Indeed, so pleased was Bishop Grandisson with his mason's craft that he wrote to Pope John XXII, 'the cathedral at Exeter, now finished up to the nave is marvellous in beauty and when completed will surpass every church of its kind in England and Wales'.

One of Exeter's treasures, the bishop's throne, is carved from Devon oak. Its canopy rises a staggering 57 ft. in height, and incorporates some of the most impressive fourteenth-century woodcarving in Europe. On the south side are two carved heads, tra-ditionally believed to be the carpenter, Robert of Galmpton and his wife. The throne was presented to the cathedral

Castleton left is a large village, magnificently sited at the western entrance to the Hope Valley. In the midst of this gentle Derbyshire countryside stands Chatsworth House above right. Built in 1707 for the 1st Duke of Devonshire, this is one of the great classical mansions of England.

Boats cast their shimmering reflections on the water at Whalley Bridge above, while the River Lathkill winds its way past Alport far left to the tumbling waterfall right.

ENGLAND

by Bishop Walter de Stapeldon two years before his death at the hands of a London mob. He was Lord High Treasurer to the ineffectual King Edward II and, as such, the figurehead of a despised ruling clique. After his assassination he was granted burial at the place of greatest honour – north of the high altar.

One interesting insight into the mediaeval mind – its need to create saints and martyrs – was exposed during the Second World War when, in May 1942, a series of devastating air raids reduced much of the city to ruin. The bombing dislodged an extraordinary collection of wax models carefully concealed within a stone cavity near the choir. They included images of animal and human limbs, a

horse's head, and the complete figure of a woman. The votive offerings represented the area requiring 'cure' and were probably placed as a mark of faith by pilgrims at the grave of the murdered Stapeldon, or upon the tomb of the highly revered Bishop, Edmund Lacy. During the Reformation the zealous dean 'cleansed' the cathedral of all such 'popish idols' and those that remained hidden over the course of three centuries owe their survival to

the stealth of some long forgotten pilgrim.

Gloucester Cathedral

Gloucester, one of the great mitred abbeys of mediaeval England (cathedral status was bestowed by King Henry VIII in 1540) owes its present splendour to the valorous decision of Abbot Thoky in 1327 to bury the mutilated remains of Edward II at his

Despite the industrial development of the northern part of the county, Warwickshire still has its 'leafy lanes' and attractive towns such as Warwick itself with its lovely Bridge End top. Imposing country homes still stand in unspoilt settings. Packwood House above, for example, with its 17th-century garden of yew trees above right which is a symbolic representation of the Sermon on the Mount.

abbey church. The mystique of kingship, allied to an association between sudden, violent death and sanctity, made this ineffectual sovereign a strange candidate for impromptu canonisation. The hitherto rare display of acumen (financed by offerings from the countless number of pilgrims that swarmed to Edward's tomb) led to the rebuilding of Gloucester Abbey in the then little known Perpendicular style – transforming the original Norman church into the birthplace of English Perpendicular Gothic architecture. Indeed, the abbey was to hold its lead in the vanguard of fashion by the beautifying of its cloisters, 1370-1412, with the earliest example of fan vaulting – unique in both extent and complexity.

Compton Wynyates left is another superb example of Tudor architecture and here too the stone and weathered brick are offset by yews and hedges tailored into neat, formal shapes.

Above is shown one of the many charming Warwickshire villages, Barton on the Heath, and overleaf the Great Hall of Warwick Castle, the finest mediaeval castle in England.

ENGLAND

Commanding an important ford over the River Severn, Gloucester is one of the most ancient of habital sites and is believed to have been founded about four thousand years ago by Iberian settlers. It was one of the great meeting places of the kingdom, remaining emphatically a royal city, closely connected to the lineage of the Old English monarchy. In the cathedral library there is a manuscript which tells how, in AD 681, King Ethelred gave Osric, a local chieftain, permission to found a monastery at Gloucester. Two centuries later King Alfred's sister, Ethelfleda, the 'lady of the Mercians' was buried on the site.

St Peter's at Gloucester, like so many Saxon abbeys, was reformed soon after the Norman invasion and Serlo, a friend and chaplain to the Conqueror, was installed as its new abbot. During thirty-three years as ruler of the House he was to earn the monks' praise as 'the walls of the church, the sword of virtue and the clarion of justice'. Construction of the existing church began in 1089 under the guidance of Abbot Serlo, who oversaw first the building of the crypt and choir and then the transepts to abut a central tower. Before the high altar lies the Conqueror's treacherous eldest son, Robert Curthose, Duke of Normandy. He was defeated and captured at the Battle of Tinchbrai by his ambitious younger brother, King Henry I, who imprisoned Robert at Cardiff Castle for twenty-eight years until his death in 1135: the body was borne to Gloucester Cathedral and there a carved oak tomb was placed over the grave; surmounted by an effigy, painted to resemble life.

The Romanesque nave at Gloucester owes the origin of its design more to Italy and Burgundy than to Normandy. It was finished by 1121, the year of its consecration and incorporates massive cylindrical columns – which are probably more awe-inspiring now than

Warwick Castle, the magnificent home of the Earls of Warwick, overlooks the River Avon above while in Welford-on-Avon above left thatched cottages offer a less imposing charm. One of the most famous of all the Warwickshire homes, Anne Hathaway's Cottage in Shottery left and right is the birthplace of Shakespeare's wife.

ENGLAND

at the date of construction, when they were brightly painted with yellows, greens and reds. This formidable but naked nave is blocked from the decorative features of the Gothic by a nineteenth-century pulpitum which permits only rare glimpses of the wonders beyond.

Few buildings demonstrate the fundamental contrast between Romanesque and late-Gothic architecture better than Gloucester Cathedral. A solid Norman nave in the former style seems to have been planned from the foundations upwards, whilst from the topmost roof the building bosses downwards in late-Gothic fashion. Such rich ornamentation was made possible by King Edward III who sent his London Court sculptors and masons to embellish the

church which housed his father's remains.

The new work at Gloucester began in 1331, only four years after Edward II's body had been received there. To permit more light and air into the dark and shadowed abbey, William of Ramsey was commissioned to advise on the new design of the transepts and choir. The solution adopted was not to pull down the existing Norman work but to clothe it with a skin of masonry in the Perpendicular style. The old roof was removed, the east end pulled down and a vast stone screen taken up the inside of the Norman arcade. Windows were inserted into the screen and a great lierne vault, 92 ft. high, erected over the whole. The apse was replaced by the Great East Window – the cathedral's chief glory

– and the largest of its kind in England. It floods the high altar with coloured light, and was paid for by Lord Bradeston and his comrade in arms, Sir Maurice Berkeley, taking as its theme the 'Coronation of the Virgin'. In the lower panels of glass, however, the valiant deeds of their fellow knights at the battle of Crécy and the siege of Calais are recorded. For this reason, the famous window (which measures 72 ft. high by 38 ft. wide) is sometimes referred to as the 'Crécy Window'.

The final flowering of the Perpendicular style – which had its birthplace here – is the Lady Chapel, com-

Stratford this page is a living tribute to the memory of Shakespeare. Overlooking the River Avon, the Royal Shakespeare Theatre above right specialises in productions of his plays, and the beautiful parish church of Holy Trinity left is Shakespeare's burial place.

North Warwickshire is dominated by Birmingham, a great industrial city, the centre of which has been given over to such modern developments as the Bullring shopping centre far left.

The vestiges of less congested days, a gracious tree walk remains in Kenilworth above left, and overleaf unique galleried shops have been preserved at the Cross in the very heart of Chester.

ENGLAND

pleted in 1499; almost its entire wall surface is filled with tall pointed glass. A similar richness adorns the 'cloisters' (a word taken from the latin 'claustrum' – an enclosed space) which possess the earliest, and possibly the finest, surviving fan vaulting. They served as a covered walkway between the various monastic buildings and acted as a place of education: indeed, Gloucester still possesses twenty 'carrels' or cells, where the monks once sat for study and meditation.

Ely Cathedral

Ely Cathedral stands as an island, its stones of ages past resting upon an isolated outcrop of Jurassic border clay, surrounded (until recently) on all sides by wild and treacherous marsh. As mists from the waters roll in to skirt

Chester, an ancient walled city on a sandstone spur north of the Dee, has preserved much of its mediaeval appearance in streets such as Eastgate Street above and left, lined with buildings dating from the Middle Ages, and in its red sandstone cathedral right, which is mainly 14th-century. Also in Cheshire, Little Moreton Hall above left, a 16th-century moated manor house, is one of the finest pieces of black-and-white architecture in England.

ENGLAND

its lower fabric, the Anglo-Norman silhouette – its immense length divided at intervals by the vertical forms of pinnacles, turrets and buttresses – rises to haunt the cowled landscape like a shadowed crown against the Fen.

The interior of the cathedral is also surmounted by a crown – a work of supreme genius and the most original conception in all mediaeval architecture – the octagon, whose very essence of spacial boldness epitomises the spirit of the Decorated style. It is a masterpiece of uplifted beauty, where light shafts downwards from the highest windows and is captured within the lantern to be held like a glorious aureola over the whole (largely Norman) body of the church.

Although the present cathedral can trace its foundation to the year 1083, the continuity of Christian worship on the Isle of Ely can be traced back over

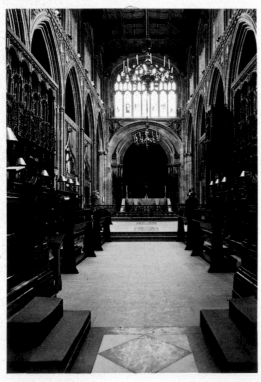

the course of thirteen centuries, to the establishment, in AD 673, of a mixed order of monks and nuns by Queen Etheldreda, who served as its first Abbess. Her sanctity and discipline gained many and distinguished converts. Persons of the noblest family, matrons of the highest rank, we are told, devoted themselves to religion under her guidance; even some of the royal estate joined her, resisting all the comforts and luxuries to which they had been accustomed, for the hard fare and severe monotony of a

monastic life; such were Etheldreda's own relatives – her sister, Sexburga, the Queen of Kent; Ermenilda, her niece and Wurburga – who succeeded each in turn to the Abbacy.

The foundress later became known as St Etheldreda (or more popularly St Audrey). She died of a throat tumour, which she interpreted as just punishment for her youthful vanity in wearing jewelled necklaces. Five-and-a-half centuries later, in 1252, King Henry III, his son Edward and a noble concourse witnessed the last translation of her relics to the sumptuous shrine in Bishop Northwood's newly built presbytery. The fame of Etheldreda depended in part on the discovery of the incorruption of her body. A chronicler writing about the event noted 'indeed her body and face appeared as fair as though she had just been dead'. During the Middle Ages a fair was held annually at Ely on the anniversary of the saint's death.

The 15th-century Perpendicular Gothic cathedral far left is one of the showpieces of Manchester.
Liverpool's Roman Catholic Metropolitan Cathedral below right was designed by Sir Frederick Gibberd and consecrated in 1967. The city's famous dockside frontage, left, above and above right extends for seven miles along the Mersey estuary, dominated by the two towers of the Royal Liver Building.

ENGLAND

The united order of monks and nuns, established and ruled over by St Etheldreda, survived as a joint order (as was the custom of the time) until the mid-tenth century. However, when St Dunstan, the reforming Archbishop of Canterbury, visited the Fens he was shocked to discover that many of the monks belonging to the great Abbey were either married or kept a mistress. Legend states that in his anger the holy man cursed all miscreants, changing them into eels – whose descendants still swarm the boggy mires and streams of East Anglia to this day; in fact, the isle's name, 'Ely', means 'place of the eels'.

The Norman Abbot, Simeon, was eighty-six years old when appointed to the See: he regarded the existing Saxon building as inadequate for the glorious worship of Christ and resolved, despite his great age, to replace it with a church of his own foundation. Thus, in 1083, began the mighty task of building the present cathedral. The choir and central tower (which proved to be ill-founded and came crashing down in 1322) were in position by the year 1106; the nave and west front (two notable survivors from the Norman Age) were completed by the late twelfth century.

The 248 ft. long Romanesque nave has twelve bays and is roughly contemporary with that at Durham. A feeling of soaring stonework is created by the exceedingly high triforium, yet the effect is no mere illusion; Ely's nave is taller than its Northumbrian counterpart – or indeed than any other Norman nave. At 86 ft. in height, however, its very nature created too many problems for a stone vault. Thus the ceiling has always been of wood; the present roof was painted by Perry and le Strange in the last century and is doubtless close to the original.

An unusual feature of the Romanesque period is to be seen at the cathedral's western end – instead of the Norman twin towers, a single tower abuts the nave and on either side flanking bays form short western transepts. The whole concept gave the west façade (with all its carved decoration and imaginative use of blind arches) a tremendous feeling of splendour and width. Sadly, the northern wing crumbled and fell away in the fifteenth century, destroying the original screening effect of the West Front and imposing its present lopsided nature.

ENGLAND

Liverpool's 'pubs' such as the Grapes *left and below left* and the Philarmonic *below* have all the distinctive atmosphere of a city which is famous for its variety of interests.

In the heart of the metropolis, Seeton Park *far left* provides a welcome retreat, while in its own quiet setting *below far left* the Anglican Cathedral, begun in 1904, forms a tribute to the design of Sir Giles Gilbert Scott.

A mixture of fact and legend surrounds the building's Norman history. The thane, Hereward the Wake – a fine soldier with a European reputation – became the leader of a mixed band of Saxon and Danish warriors who flocked to his battle standard. In the autumn months of 1069 they took refuge on the Isle of Ely and, protected on all sides by uncharted marshes, converted Ely Abbey into a fortress from which they launched a campaign of resistance against the Norman aggressors. King William and his army lay siege to the island yet, despite being hopelessly outnumbered, the warriors made one last defiant stand for the Saxon cause. The besieging army constructed a causeway across the swamp from Aldreth to Ely, the narrowest crossing. As the Normans prepared to attack, Hereward managed to set fire to the timber causeway and, fanned by strong winds, the flames raged through the reed-beds striking panic into the Norman vanguard. Goaded by showers of arrows and blinded by thick, choking smoke, they fled into the marshes and perished in their hundreds. The defeat was a spur to William and by 1071 the Abbey was in Norman hands – betrayed by the starving monks who, in return for amnesty, led William's army to the isle

ENGLAND

by way of a secret path through the almost impenetrable swamps.

In 1109 the See of Ely was created, torn from the southern episcopal domain of Lincoln. The posts of both Bishop and Abbot were combined to give one trusted man – Hervé le Breton and his successors – the control of civil jurisdiction (as at Durham) in order that he might better guard against future Anglo-Saxon resistance. The building programme flourished under Ely's Norman bishops and the cathedral masons were fortunate in being permitted access to the stone pits of Barnak, where the hardest limestone in England was quarried. The exceptional durability of the stone has preserved the quality of carving and some of the finest Norman sculpture survives at Ely. The Prior's door, circa 1150, is a Romanesque masterpiece noted for the carving of 'Christ in Glory' hewn from its limestone tympanum; the flat linear tones of the sculpture owe much to the influence of English manuscript illustration whilst its abstract vitality is an odious legacy of Viking art.

Bishop Hugh of Northwood's choir and presbytery were built by extending eastwards beyond the Norman apse to provide a more

Blackpool these pages is a holiday town which began to develop as a recreational resort in the mid-18th century, and which has gained steadily in popularity ever since. The famous promenade is dominated by the 518 ft. Blackpool Tower which contains the ballroom above. Every autumn sees the illumination of decorations along the shore, and the pleasure beach on the South Shore, known as the 'Golden Mile' left, is packed with funfair attractions.

Sunset enhances the quiet splendour of Derwentwater overleaf.

ENGLAND

adequate setting for St Etheldreda's shrine. It was constructed during the period 1234-1252, and the dignity and simplicity of the building clearly belongs to the Early English style. Slender piers of Barnak stone are surrounded by eight shafts of polished marble which rise to stiff-leaf capitals and dog-tooth ornamentation. Contemporary with the choir is the delicately worked Galilee porch which projects from the West Front, a gift of Bishop Eustace. From its entrance, the whole 537 ft. length of the building is impressively visible. The eye passes along the slow solemn rhythm of the vast nave and through the liveliness of the choir to alight upon the great stained glass window beyond the high altar.

The foundations of a Lady Chapel were laid at the Festival of the Annunciation in 1321 but less than a year later a disaster occurred at Ely which halted its progress and was destined to have a far-reaching effect upon the cathedral. Shortly after Matins on 22nd February the central tower collapsed 'with a roar like thunder, of

The Lake District includes some of the wildest and most majestic of England's countryside, yet nestled beneath the bold austerity of the crags are superb lakes like Derwentwater right, *Crummock Water* far right *and Haweswater* overleaf, *and sweeping valleys dotted with isolated farms* above. *The environs of the central lakes have changed little since the days when Wordsworth explored scenery such as that near Tarn Hows* above right *from his home at Grasmere* above far right.

shock and so great a tumult'. Where once had stood the massive Norman building, there was now but a gaping hole torn from the very heart of the cathedral. Faced with this disaster the sacrist, Alan of Walsingham (a man of unusual vision), decided against restoring the tower, opting instead for the daringly experimental idea of constructing an octagon.

The mediaeval passion for geometry created the breathtaking purity of the octagon, erected by the most distin-

guished craftsman of his age, the King's Master Carpenter, William Hurle, whose imaginative powers matched those of the design. Instead of re-erecting the four piers which had supported the tower, the sacrist chose instead to demolish the four aisle bays at each corner, thus transforming the crossing from a square into an octagon. After searching the realm for trees of the appropriate size, he finally settled for eight massive baulks of oak brought from Chicksand in Bedford-

ENGLAND

shire, each weighing 10 tons. These were trimmed to 64 ft. in length and positioned to form the corner posts of the new building, leaning inwards to meet as a ring beneath the lantern window. When completed, the whole downward thrust rested solely on these eight pillars.

The 70 ft. span was too wide for a stone roof so the vault was constructed of timber to lessen the load. Built upon a hammer and beam principle (of which this is one of the earliest examples), the main elements of the design were adapted by William Hurle to suit the polygonal plan. By using the great upright oak beams of the octagon as hammer posts he created a domed pattern which, from the ground, echoes a star-shaped vault. At its centre the lantern rises a further 60 ft., lit by traceried windows which flood the crossing with dappled light. At the base of the eight arches are

carved the heads of those involved in its construction – Alan of Walsingham, William Hurle, King Edward III, Queen Philippa, Bishop Hotham and Prior Crauden.

In the mid 1330's work resumed on the Lady Chapel under the direction of the monk, John of Wisbeach, who succeeded in creating the largest chapel of its kind in England. Emphasis is placed upon width rather than height. Its roof span of 46 ft. marks the widest unsupported mediaeval vault. However, its construction is so delicate that the middle of the span is only 18 inches

higher than that of the sides. The sense of space is enhanced by the motif of nodding ogee arches (pointed arches of double curvature, convex above concave) which align the walls to form seats or niches. Their canopies are carved from a local hard chalk, known as clunch, which is suitable for astonishingly fine sculptured detail, as witness the wealth of carved foliage reminiscent of bladder-wrack seaweed or dried oak leaves. The Lady Chapel marks the end of full-scale construction. Fortunately for Ely, the cathedral was completed immediately before the Black Death, whose evil

sickle claimed one person in every three and so disastrously brought to an end the marvellous advances of fourteenth-century architecture.

Wordsworth pronounced his home village of Grasmere 'the loveliest spot that man hath ever found' but the description could be applied to a number of the many beauty spots in Cumberland and Westmorland – to Elterwater below, Great Langdale far left, Bowness right or Derwentwater below right.

ENGLAND

Durham

Considered to be the world's supreme masterpiece of Romanesque architecture, the Anglo-Norman Cathedral at Durham could want for no finer setting. It dominates the lofty outcrop of sandstone on which it rests, encircled on three sides by a great loop of the River Wear and guarded on its landward approach by a mighty Norman fortress. The strength of its position made Durham the 'Citadel of the Holy Church of the North', shielding the many relics of its saints against the ravages of Scottish incursion. It is the only city near the border never to have fallen into their hands, earning it the proud description 'half house of God, half castle 'gainst the Scots'.

The beauty and drama of the cathedral's exterior (unrivalled by any other) is magnificently enhanced upon entering within. The spirit of the place is one of might and overwhelming grandeur. The lofty nave arcading is borne on alternating clustered piers and massive, circular columns – each boldly incised with swirling, almost barbaric, patterns of chevron, vertical flute and chequered diaper. Above the aisle, shadowed galleries harbour England's first flying buttresses, which date from 1133. The cathedral is also the earliest building in Europe to have ribbed vaults throughout and pioneered the use of pointed, transverse arches to divide the nave into bays. Although such features were to become a prominent architectural

Since time immemorial sheep have grazed on the Yorkshire moors and the wool trade has made Leeds, with its fine civic hall above, the world centre for ready-made clothing. York is famous for its old city walls left which gird the ancient city for three miles, while Knaresborough below is noted for its river Nidd.

The North Riding coast is punctuated with fishing ports and seaside towns such as Whitby below right, dominated by the abbey ruins above right, and Scarborough overleaf, crowned by the remains of a 12th-century castle. At Robin Hood's Bay below left, red-roofed cottages jostle for the sea front.

ENGLAND

feature, the spirit of Durham is not in the slightest degree Gothic.

The stones here laid can trace their origins to the first Norman bishops, yet the site has a living presence which links Durham to one man – a 'low' shepherd with a burning vocation to serve God. He was Cuthbert, whose saintly remains proved inspiration for the founding of the cathedral, and whose shrine was to become the 'brightest jewel' of the north. On the night of 31st August AD 651, as Saint Aidan lay dying in the parish church at Bamburgh, a fair-headed youth stood watch over the sheep on the Lammermuir hills; here Cuthbert witnessed a vision of angels, holding a shining soul, as they ascended toward the heavens. On learning of Aidan's death some days later, he interpreted the vision and vowed to dedicate the rest of his life to God.

Thirteen years he spent travelling the lands north of the Roman wall and many legends became associated with him: seals were said to dry his feet with their fur; and at the Isle of Coquet two hideous sea monsters rose from the water's depths to kneel before him and be blessed. As Cuthbert's reputation for spiritual insight and holiness

SH28.

PROGRESSIVE

ENGLAND

travelled before him, so his fame increased. He was appointed Prior to Lindisfarne and, although he served his community well, the solitary spirit of the Celtic tradition began to assert itself and he eventually withdrew to the lonely Farne Isles to live the life of a hermit. For nine years he dwelt in a sunken cell, encircled by a high wall of turf so that neither the land nor the sea could draw his gaze away from heaven. Eventually, in AD 685, Cuthbert reluctantly allowed himself to be consecrated Bishop of Lindisfarne, on condition that after his death his bones 'should rest but amongst Christians'.

In AD 875 a devastating series of Viking attacks (forecast by the portents of storms and fiery serpents seen in the skies above Holy Island) forced the community to flee to the mainland, taking with them Cuthbert's mortal remains – in fulfilment of their pledge. According to legend, the monks were instructed in a dream to seek the safety of the 'Dunholme'; upon waking they happened to hear a milkmaid speak of it as a place where her cow had strayed. Thus guided, the Lindisfarne brethren built a small chapel 'of

In York below old timber-framed houses lean towards each other across the narrow Shambles while, on the coast, the harbour of Whitby bottom is ringed by a fishing village of steep alleyways and hillside cottages.

Inland Yorkshire is dominated by the Dales and windswept countryside like the surroundings of Malham below right, protected by low stone walls and dotted with isolated farms below left and villages such as Muker right.

wands and branches' on a rocky plateau (where now stands the cathedral), around which the wooded gorge of the River Wear describes an elongated horseshoe. A century later, in AD 999 – a year of grim foreboding when many men awaited the end of the world – the monks of Durham found prosperity and peace. They began constructing the 'White Church', of which

only admiring descriptions now remain.

Upon the Conqueror's arrival in England, the era of the great territorial Lordship of the bishops of Durham was dawning. The first Norman King immediately recognised the importance of the site and built a castle nearby – firstly to subjugate the rebellious Saxons of the north and later to

create a bulwark against the Scots. By transferring the Earldom of Northumberland into the hands of the bishops, the authority of the Palatine of Durham stretched from the River Tees to the Tyne. It was an area where the 'King's writ did not run', and where the immense power of the Prince-Bishop was elevated to that of a temporal ruler with his own coinage and

parliament. In return, for special concessions and privileges, the crown demanded acts of loyalty – notably against the Scots. Under St Cuthbert's banner (made from part of his shroud) many famous 'warrior-bishops' – notably Antony Beck and Thomas of Hatfield – led their armies northwards. Indeed, anthems are still sung from the top of the cathedral's central tower on the 29th May each year, to commemorate the deliverance of Neville's Cross, when one such English army spectacularly repelled the Scottish invasion of 1346.

Durham's first Norman bishop met his death at the hands of a mob early in his reign. His successor, Bishop William de St Carilef, was fortunate not to suffer a similar fate: he was accused of plotting against his sovereign, William Rufus, and was lucky to escape with a sentence of banishment. During his three years of exile the Bishop must have seen the new churches of France and Burgundy and decided to create a similar feeling of majesty in his own cathedral at Durham. Thus the Saxon 'white church' – less than a century old – was destroyed to make way for what was destined to become the masterpiece of its age.

On the 11th August 1093 the foundations were laid by Bishop William and Prior Turgot. King Malcolm III of Scotland (who defeated and slew Macbeth) was a guest at the ceremony. Within the remarkably short time of forty years the construction was finished. Most of the present cathedral dates from the period 1093-1133, standing to this day vast and impressive in its massive strength and yet so well proportioned that nothing about it seems ponderous.

The 201 ft. long nave was considered the miracle of its day. The massive sandstone pillars are decidedly Norman, emphatically structural in nature, yet high above, the arches form points – a device developed by the twelfth-century masons at Durham to bring light into the church. This is the first appearance of the pointed arch in Europe – a feature that was to be the secret of the world's greatest architecture – Durham is thus not merely the triumphant climax of Romanesque art but also the first hint of Gothic.

As the cathedral soared above the castle at its side, the much travelled body of St Cuthbert found a final

ENGLAND

resting place at the heart of England's strongest citadel of the Faith. The shrine itself was 'exalted with the most curious workmanship, of fine and costly green marble, all limned (painted) with gilt and gold; having four seats underneath the shrine for lame men to offer their devout and fervent prayer to God and Holy St Cuthbert, for his miraculous relief and succour which, being never wanting, made the shrine to be so richly invested with silver, gold, elephant tooth and suchlike things, that it was esteemed one of the most fabled monuments in all England'. Of the many gifts that crowded the shrine, amongst the most unusual were part of Moses' rod, a fragment of the Lord's manger, a unicorn horn and the claw of a griffon (another mystical beast) with several of her eggs. Only men were admitted to the presence of the tomb as St Cuthbert appears to have developed an aversion to women, which in mediaeval times resulted in the defining of a black, frostily marbled boundary over which no female dared tread.

The fortunes of Durham wavered in the fifteenth century, for we are told that in 1429 the cathedral tower was struck by lightning, and the monks were apparently too poor to meet the rebuilding costs. Prior John of Wessington (or Washington: for he

came from the family which later gave America its first President) sent his brethren out into the world to beg for money, armed only with a silver crucifix and a piece of cloth from St Cuthbert's shroud. The relics failed to stir the people of the Palatine to pious generosity for nothing was done about the tower until 1455, by which time it was in serious danger of collapse. The central tower was eventually restored

Yorkshire is rich in ecclesiastical architecture and York is second only to Norwich in the number of old churches included within its limits, among them its splendid Minster right and the ruins of St Mary's above. Rievaulx Abbey left is one of the earliest Cistercian buildings in England.

in 1499, thus bringing to an end four centuries of building.

One final sequel to the rich tapestry of Durham's past occurred in 1540, when the King's agents stormed into the cathedral intent upon despoiling the 'popish' shrine and destroying all evidence of the saint. To their amazement, when they opened Cuthbert's tomb they found his body – despite the passing of eight centuries – to be in perfect condition with no visible signs of decay. To the monks, however, it was common knowledge that the saint's hair and nails had continued to grow and, from time to time, it was necessary for the guardian of the shrine to open the tomb and trim their growth. At the discretion of the commission, Durham's chief treasure was allowed to rest beneath the site of his once sumptuous shrine, under a grey slab of stone simply inscribed 'Cuthbertus'.

Durham Cathedral above right, standing on a 70ft rock surrounded on three sides by the River Wear, was begun in 1093 by the Norman bishop, William of Calais.

Just off the Northumbrian coast, on Holy Island, the castle of Lindisfarne above and right perches on an equally steep rock. This small stronghold has presided over the island since the 16th century.

The product of more recent engineering, the New Tyne Bridge left is one of five bridges which span the Tyne at Newcastle.

CRAFTS

Craftsmanship is alive and well, and thriving in almost every part of the country. True, some crafts are dying out, but far fewer than might be imagined. The heartening fact is that new crafts are gradually emerging to take the place of some of the old, and there is no lack of younger people wanting to play their part in continuing the long tradition of craftsmanship of which we in Britain can be so proud. Whether this point could have been made a few years ago is debatable. It seems almost as though we are slowly emerging from a long tunnel in which mass-production reigned supreme; a narrow, throw-away society in which built-in obsolescence was the order of the day. To a very large extent we are, and will remain, in the tunnel, but at least people are now beginning to question the values of the society in which they find themselves. Advertisers are by no means slow to spot trends and changes, indeed their very livelihood can depend on their ability to foresee them. It can be no matter of chance, therefore, that we now find ourselves surrounded by exhortations as to the 'home-made' quality or 'country-fresh' flavour or atmosphere of one product or another. However spurious any or all of these claims may or may not be, they do reflect a desire on the part of a growing number of people for something that at least sounds, and looks, genuine – and may even be so!

In the past, in many of the crafts carried on in rural areas, there was an inevitable overlapping of skills. This was particularly true, and is so today, of the wheelwright, who had to combine the skills of advanced carpentry with those of the blacksmith, adding his own particular expertise.

Dennis Flower, of Farmborough, is pictured on this page repairing and reconstructing old wheels and producing new.

CRAFTS

There was a time, of course, when all things were hand-made. They were then, presumably, either considered well-made or poorly-made and the fact that they were hand-crafted didn't enter into it. We have now reached the stage where the fact that something is hand-made is, in itself, cause for comment and we must re-learn to distinguish, surely on the basis of the article fulfilling its function, between the good and the not so good. It would be quite wrong to encourage craftsmanship for the wrong reasons and to accept a poorly made product as good only because it is hand-made or 'original'. That way lies a cheapening of craftsmanship and a denial of its very name.

Crafts are entered into for a variety of reasons. Certainly in the case of rural crafts in the old days it was in most instances a matter of following the family tradition. If your father was a blacksmith or a chair-maker then the odds were that you would follow in his footsteps in much the same way that sons followed their fathers into the coal mines, or the mills and factories, in industrial areas. Things have changed greatly now and there is no longer the traditional compulsion to follow in anyone's footsteps. We can,

It seems not so many years ago that there were farriers above in every town and village in the British Isles. Their numbers are now, of course, fewer, but it is a craft that may still be seen and for which there is still a surprisingly large demand.

Thatch above right – straw or reeds used as a roof over a dwelling – is one of the oldest methods of providing shelter against the elements.

Joe Bonham has been hand-crafting his St Leonard fishing rods for customers both here and overseas for over fifty years, using skills taught him by his grandfather – who also taught him that there are only two ways to do a job – the right way and the wrong way.

Before starting work on a new rod he carefully selects top a length of seasoned Tonkin bamboo for splitting.

CRAFTS

to a large extent, choose the job or profession we wish. It would seem unlikely, however, that anyone would decide to take up a craft, and make it their life's work purely for the money they would get out of it. A very few craftsmen do make large sums of money, but most of them do not. They make a living, and what they do not gain in financial rewards is, they feel, compensated by their freedom to do what they want without any – or with very little – interference from outside. This wish to achieve some measure of individual freedom is certainly one of the factors that many craftsmen and women take into consideration, particularly those who work entirely alone. There is also the strong desire to do something in their own way, something they feel they will be good at and eventually become masters of.

The problem a craftsman faces when it comes to the question of deciding on a price for his product, or a fee for his services, can be a very difficult one. If he or she was to charge the customer, on a basis of time alone, at the average

Just a few of the many lasts left stored in the basements of one of the oldest of London's hand-made shoemakers, John Lobb of St James's. Customers represented can order another pair of made-to-measure shoes without calling for a fitting.

Top left and top centre: Bob Tarling at work in his pottery. There is a peaceful fascination in watching as the beauty and symmetry of the pot emerges from the wet clay in the potter's hands.

Above left, above and top: Since the latter half of the 19th century the majority of pipes have been fashioned from the briar, a species of heather found in the Mediterranean area.

CRAFTS

Oak for barrels is now both difficult to obtain and very expensive. For this reason the greater part of the cooper's time is now spent on repairs or in producing 're-made' barrels, as at Tom Wright's cooperage bottom left in Surrey.

Clockmaking and repairing are skills not easily learnt, and Michael Potter below served a long apprenticeship with the holders of the Royal Warrant, Charles Frodsham and Company.

Busy machinery bottom at Newalls Tweed Mills, Stornoway, Isle of Lewis.

Above and right: the Gandolfi's have been making the cameras that bear their name since the 1880s. These superbly fashioned yet highly functional instruments are now crafted by the last surviving members of the family, Frederick and Arthur Gandolfi, from the same beautiful materials as always – Spanish mahogany, Honduras mahogany, teak and hand-cut and lacquered brass fittings.

CRAFTS

hourly rate paid by industry throughout the country, then it would put the price up to an unacceptably high level. The problem is that, in our age of mass-produced units, so few people realise, looking at a genuine hand-made article, just how much time went into its making, and this is without taking into account the many years that may have been spent in perfecting the necessary skills in order to produce it. The reverse of the problem is that if too low a price is charged, then the product tends to be regarded as too cheap, and therefore not worth buying for its intrinsic value as opposed to its practical worth, and the craftsman finds that he cannot make a living.

There are, in this country, organisations whose purpose is to assist and encourage, in many different ways, the growth and prosperity of craftsmanship and craftsmen. The Crafts Advisory Committee maintains a selective list of craftsmen whose work is illustrated in a library of colour slides. Many of these are available on loan for lectures or other purposes which will promote interest in various crafts and help to ensure that the craftsman's work is made known, and sold, to as wide a section of the public as possible.

CoSIRA – the Council for Small Industries in Rural Areas – is another such organisation. To quote from one of their publications . . . "CoSIRA is an advisory and credit service, sponsored by the government, to assist small firms in rural areas of England and Wales. Its aim is to help small firms to become more prosperous and so provide more employment in the countryside. If the firm is a manufacturing or service industry or business, employing not more than twenty skilled persons, and is situated in a rural area or in a country town with a population of ten thousand or less, then it is eligible." Both these organisations publish a comprehensive index of craftsmen and, in the case of CoSIRA, craft shops.

Spinets, harpsichords, clavichords and pianos. The name of Morley has been connected with music and musical instruments in one form or another for over three hundred and fifty years, the family having established themselves as musical instrument makers in the City of London in Regency times.

The importance of craft shops should not be underestimated. They are, quite often, the only contact the craftsman has with the public, other than selling direct, and the placing of products in carefully selected outlets can obviously do much to assist him in placing work before the public, therefore allowing him to concentrate on what he does best.

Most good craft shops are quite knowledgeable about craftsmen in their area and will usually be only too pleased to put potential customers in touch with craftsmen whose specialised services they require.

It seems that we are rather apt, in this country, to denigrate our achievements, and particularly to question our own capacity for hard work. Visiting craftsmen at work in various parts of the country, and in widely different fields, however, it would be hard to come to any other conclusion than that we are quite wrong in making such an assumption. What seems to be at the root of the problem may well be a peculiarity of the British character. It seems

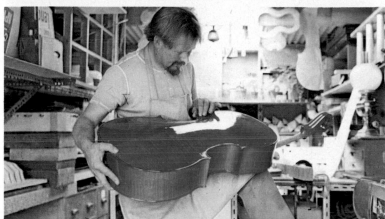

Julian Emery is a violin, viola and cello maker. He is pictured this page in his workshop at his home in a peaceful Wiltshire village. Stringed instruments, their construction and the music played on them, form a large part of Julian Emery's life. He studied the violin before deciding to make them as a hobby and then spent some time as a violin repairer before making the decision to concentrate full-time on their construction.

CRAFTS

Top left: *an old cider press at Wedmore in Somerset. Centre left: thatching nearing completion on a Somerset cottage. Left: Archie Harris thatching a bird house at Blagdon, Somerset. Top: dyed leather for cricket ball covers drying naturally at Alfred Reader's, Teston, Kent, and the finished product above being inspected. Right: an old Aran craftsman making a basket. Opposite page, left: Stuart King, maker of miniature chairs, in his fascinating workshop in Buckinghamshire. Far right: Sussex trug baskets being constructed at Hurstmonceux.*

that if we are left alone to do a job that interests us, that we consider worthwhile, and resulting from which we can perceive our part in an end product in which we can take pride, then we seem to have an infinite capacity for both hard work and good workmanship. If, on the other hand, we are regimented, formed into large, impersonal groups and expected to do a job we neither fully understand nor see the purpose of, then we are inclined to rebel, to lose what little interest we had, and to look for ways of avoiding it. Perhaps the mass-production methods of other countries are just not suited to our individual and independent nature.

WALES

Some of the most impressive scenery in the whole of Great Britain can be found in Wales: land of magnificent mountains and gentle valleys, charming mountain streams and cascading waterfalls, spectacular passes, remote, wood-fringed lakes, green undulating hills and heather-clad moors.

The backbone of Wales, and the heart of the magnificent scenery, is the Cambrian Mountains, and Mount Snowdon at 3,560 ft is the highest mountain in Great Britain south of the Scottish border. From Roman times Snowdonia has attracted climbers eager to accept the challenge of the rugged and dangerous rock faces and in the 18th and 19th centuries artists were frequent visitors, inspired by the breathtaking landscapes which remain unspoilt today.

The Cambrian Mountains, together with the Brecon Beacons and the Black Mountains, form an integral part of Welsh history. For centuries they acted as an effective barrier against invaders, but in turn the Romans, Normans and Plantagenets broke through, all eager to rule the strong-willed Celtic inhabitants of this relatively isolated part of Britain. These different cultures left their individual marks on Wales: the Romans built roads and fortresses and the legionary camp at Carleon, Gwent; the Normans built the solid castles of Chepstow and Pembroke and the Plantagenets built the fine castles of Caernarvon, Beaumaris and Harlech, under the direction of King Edward I. It was he who established English rule over Wales for the first time, in 1282 – 4. His son, who was born at Caernarvon, was created the first Prince of Wales, in 1301.

The beauty of Wales lies not only in its mountains and valleys. The county of Dyfed, south-west Wales, has a dramatic, weather-beaten coastline, with high cliffs and sandy bays.

Llanberis Pass left is the idyllic haunt of enthusiastic mountain climbers attracted by the majesty of Llyn Peris and Llyn Padarn.

WALES

Delightful resorts such as Tenby and St David's make it a favoured holiday area. St David's, named after the patron saint of Wales, is the smallest cathedral city in Britain.

In south-east Dyfed lies the town of Carmarthen, which is said to have been the birthplace of the legendary wizard, Merlin. It was believed that he cast a spell on an oak tree in Priory Street, declaring that if it should ever fall, so would the town. Such is the strength of legend that the rotting stump can be seen today, embedded in concrete and supported by iron bands!

One of the most attractive towns in Dyfed is undoubtedly Laugharne, with its old castle and picturesque harbour. It was here that the famous Welsh poet, Dylan Thomas, lived for many years. Several of his poems were written in the tiny, remote cottage by the waterside, overlooking the magnificent hills, and it is the town of Laugharne and its inhabitants on which 'Under Milk Wood' is believed to have been based.

Conwy Castle, Gwynedd **right** *casts a formidable silhouette against the last light of the setting sun.*

The design of Caernarvon Castle **left, above left and above** *with its different coloured masonry has suggested a resemblance to the walls of Constantinople, and the idea has been put forward that Edward I intended it to form a visible link with the old Welsh legend which holds that this was the birthplace of the Emperor Constantine. The castle, which stands on the Menai Strait facing Anglesey, was the birthplace of Edward, son of Edward I, who was destined to become the Prince of Wales.*

Off the coast are several craggy islands which are inhabited only by vast numbers of seabirds and seals. Grassholme Island, just 12 miles offshore, is one of the largest gannetries in the world, with more than 15,000 pairs of gannets nesting there.

A characteristic of the northern part of Dyfed is the extensive, sweeping moorlands and the magnificent coastline. The River Teifi is a

The most recent investiture at Caernarvon Castle above left was, of course, that of Prince Charles this page, who was invested as Prince of Wales by Her Majesty the Queen in 1969.

So effectively does Telford's suspension bridge blend with Conwy Castle left that it is difficult to imagine that six centuries elapsed between their construction.

The SMALLEST HOUSE In GREAT BRITAIN

At any time

The Smallest House
in Great Britain.

ADMISSION 3
NOT OPEN ON SUNDAYS

haven for salmon and trout anglers and the art of fishing from coracles is still practised. These tub-shaped boats have been used since the time of the Ancient Britons and except for canvas in place of hide to cover the wicker frames, the design has remained unchanged. There is little industry in this area but many of the traditional crafts, such as weaving and woodcarving,

In Conwy Quay, Gwynedd stands the smallest house in Britain left with its two tiny rooms linked by a staircase. The longest station sign in Britain below is now housed in the museum at Penrhyn Castle. Mercifully shortened to Llanfair P.G., even the romantic meaning of 'The church of St Mary by the hollow of white aspen, over the whirlpool and St Tysilio's church close to the red cave' is somewhat daunting.

The narrow gauge Ffestiniog Railway Station right, originally built to carry the slate from the quarries to Portmadoc, was reopened for passengers in 1954 and runs from Portmadoc to Dduallt.

LLANFAIRPWLLGWYNGYLLGOGERYCHWYRNDROBWYLL-LLANTYSILIOGOGOGOCH
RAILWAY STATION

CAFE

WALES

prosper here as well as in other parts of the country.

Industry developed mostly in Glamorgan, and has left its mark on the once green and peaceful valleys of the Brecon Beacons. Pontypridd, Neath and Rhondda are the locations of the numerous unsightly iron and coal mines that have given employment to many in the last 150 years whilst resulting in the destruction of much of the surrounding beauty. Today, however, work is being done to recover the scarred countryside by the clearing of tips and planting of trees.

The largest city in Glamorgan and the capital of Wales since 1955 is Cardiff, the great seaport on the Bristol Channel. It rose to prosperity with the building of the first dock in 1839 and the subsequent export of coal. Today it is a modern industrial city with many docks and factories. Its large stadium, Cardiff Arms Park, is

Scenes such as those shown on this page have drawn innumerable holidaymakers to the coast of the lovely county of Gwynedd, and Conwy above left is understandably one of its most popular resorts.

The beach scene above was photographed at Morfa Nefyn, another much loved haunt, while left the low-lying island of Anglesey is the dramatic setting for South Stack Lighthouse, poised on its menacing rocks.

WALES

the Mecca for supporters of Welsh rugby football.

In common with many of the counties of Wales, Glamorgan has numerous lovely beaches, particularly between Barry and Porthcawl. The Gower Peninsula, too, is a restful retreat from the industrial suburbs, and here the cockle gatherers of Penclawdd can be `seen, driving their ponies and donkeys across the treacherous sands of the silted-up Loughor Estuary, to the prized cockle-beds.

The island of Anglesey is linked to the mainland of Wales by Telford's spectacular suspension bridge left.

Dolgellau, Gwynedd below, lies in a long valley which has become a popular centre for touring in Wales, even in winter when snow lies on the surrounding hills.

WALES

Bounded on the south by the Bristol Channel and to the east by England, is the county of Gwent. It was here that Caractacus and his Silurian tribes fought against the invading Romans. In later years the Normans, struggling hard to maintain control over this border country, constructed stalwart castles. Although in ruins today, Chepstow Castle still commands an impressive position over the River Wye and the mediaeval streets of the old market town. Close by are the remains of Tintern Abbey, a monastery founded by the Cistercian order of monks who were suppressed by Henry VIII in 1536. The Abbey has been described as the jewel of the Wye valley, so outstanding is its setting, and has

The Dyfed coast from Camarthen Bay to Cardigan Bay provides some magnificent scenery right as well as some very attractive little cliff-top villages such as Tresaith below.

A shepherd drives his sheep below right through the wet bracken of a leafy lane at Dolgoch, deep in the Cader Idris mountain country. Harlech Castle left was completed by Edward I in the 13th century. It was the last stronghold of the Lancastrians in North Wales and also the last held by the Royalists in the Civil War.

The Italian village of Portofino inspired the Welsh architect Clough Williams-Ellis to create his dream in stone below far right . . . Portmeirion.

WALES

been the source of much artistic inspiration for both painters and poets.

Now a part of the larger region of Powys, the old county of Radnor, characterised by its large expanses of moorland and isolated hills, was so sparsely populated that sheep outnumbered people. The area is known for its old spa towns, such as Builth Wells and Llangammarch Wells and its reservoirs provide soft, Welsh water for Birmingham.

The bustling town of Welshpool, in the north-east of Powys, is renowned for its outstanding Georgian architecture. The showpiece of the town, however, is Powys Castle, built in 1250. The gardens were formulated in the 18th century by the celebrated Capability Brown, and include a 181 ft high Douglas Fir, which is reputedly the tallest tree in Britain.

WALES

One of the areas most frequented by holiday makers is the northern coast of Wales. The large resorts of Colwyn Bay, Llandudno and Rhyl and the smaller ones on the pretty island of Anglesey are popular for sunbathing and swimming, especially with people from nearby Merseyside, and there are plenty of places of interest to visit in the beautiful surrounding countryside should the sun not shine.

The Welsh people's intense pride in their country and language is nowhere better illustrated than in the many Eisteddfods that are staged every year. Their love of singing and dancing, and writing and speaking their musical language, reaches out to inspire all who go to watch and listen.

Aberaeron above is a splendid little holiday spot, ideally situated at the mouth of the Afon Aeron.

The City Hall above left is that of Cardiff, the capital of Wales and an important port on the Bristol Channel as well as a University City. The Castle left dates from Norman times and was once the home of the Bute family.

Pembroke Castle's walls above right formerly encircled the town and today they still add a romantic atmosphere.

The ruins of the 12th to 14th-century Cistercian Abbey right stand in a secluded wooded setting by a curve in the River Wye.

SCOTLAND

Scotland and England have been ruled by the same monarchy, and governed by the same parliament, for well over 250 years. The inhabitants of both countries speak the same language and use the same currency. They don't need passports or visas to move from one country to the other and there are no customs posts on the border. Yet when most Englishmen cross the border into Scotland there is a very definite feeling of entering a foreign country. It is the 'Scottishness' of Scotland that sets any first-time visitor back on his heels.

'You see it in the architecture', says Michael Powell in Alastair MacLean's Scotland (Deutsch 1972), 'in the colossal granite walls of Aberdeen, in the majestic sweep into the heart of Dundee of the road bridge over the Tay, in the fantasies of Scottish baronial, in the purity of the Brothers Adam. You hear it in the speech – direct, literate and colourful – whether broad Lowland or careful Highland. You enjoy it in the abundance of public golf courses; the stupendous high teas; the generous drams of whisky; the electric blankets on the clean beds; the unpretentious goodness of the small things in life.'

You see it, too, in the breathtaking sweep of a Highland glen, where the thin winding ribbon of grey road creeping almost apologetically through it seems a concession of nature to man's intrusion. The delicate hues of bracken and heather on either side of the road are broken by a mountain stream that was bubbling when Scotland had its own kings, and a Sassenach Englishman took his life in his hands if he crossed the border. And you see it in the fickle-tempered islands off the west coast – tranquil and loving one day, angry and violent the next. The people who live there are primarily small farmers and fishermen who exist largely as their forefathers did, living a hard but rich life wedded utterly to the land they work or the sea they fish.

The untarnished gold of a sunset over an inland loch left or the exhilarating sound of traditional pipers overleaf are very much part of the wild beauty associated with Scotland.

SCOTLAND

It is the Scots themselves who have given their land this unique sense of identity – no mean achievement for a country of just over five million people. It has been argued that the Scots have produced more eminent figures per capita than any other people. More than half the total number of American Presidents have Scottish ancestry and many British Prime Ministers have been Scots: Macmillan, Douglas-Home, Gladstone, Ramsay Mac-Donald. Menzies of Australia and Fraser of New Zealand also had Scottish blood and John Paul Jones, founder of the US Navy, was a Scot. And in many other fields, Scots are internationally acclaimed; Andrew Carnegie, Adam Smith, James Watt, Robert Burns and Sir Walter Scott, to

Lapped by the gentle Gulf Stream, the glorious promontory of the Mull of Galloway left is part of a rich store of beauty in scenic Wigtownshire. Portpatrick top and centre right, to the north of the Mull, was once a 'Gretna Green' for the Irish, who would sail the 21 miles from Donaghadee to be married there.

South of the Royal Burgh of Dumfries on the banks of the River Nith bottom right, stands the 14th-century sandstone castle of Caerlaverock below.

SCOTLAND

name but a few. But the irony is that so many Scots achieved their success after leaving their homeland, making their mark on the world in foreign fields.

But where did the Scots come from originally? Most historians agree that the first man to stand upright on the rugged terrain of what is now Scotland did so perhaps as long ago as 6,000 BC. Bone and antler fishing spears and other rudimentary implements found mainly along the western part of the country serve as evidence to support this theory.

The Beaker civilisation arrived three thousand years later, and lived mainly in henges. They spread as far north as Orkney, and as far south as Dumfries.

It was not for another 1,500 years or so that the first signs of Scotland's Celtic origins appeared. Around 500 BC the sparse population was roughly divided into two distinct areas. In the north and west, living in 'duns' and

Grey Mare's Tail above, one of Scotland's highest waterfalls, is sited 8½ miles north-east of Moffat in the spectacular hill country of Annandale. Part of the country's rich historical legacy, the heart of Robert the Bruce is buried beneath the high altar of Melrose Abbey right, and Abbotsford House above right was for many years the home of Sir Walter Scott and the scene of his death in 1832.

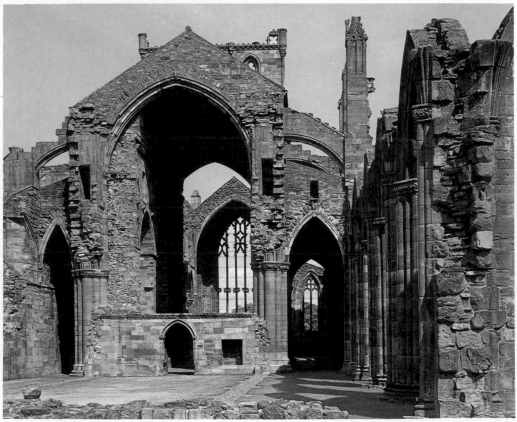

'brochs', were the people who became known as Picts. To the south and east, mainly in hill forts and camps, lived the Britons who called their land Alba. One of their chief settlements was Din Eidyn (Edinburgh).

The Roman Invasion of Britain isolated the two peoples even further. The Britons capitulated before the Roman legions and over the years of the occupation learned to work with them. The Picts, however, never bowed to Rome and even Hadrian's Wall was not strong enough to keep them from attacking the settlements to the south. As the Roman grip weakened, toward the end of the fourth century, their forces abandoned any hope of suppressing the Picts and, instead, appointed local Briton chiefs to uphold the law, such as it was.

The Irish Connection

But the Picts and the Britons were not the forerunners of the Scots of today. Scotland's heritage, in fact, came from Ireland in the 6th century, with an exodus of Gaels looking for fresh pastures. They landed in Argyll and, when the Irish St Columba followed a few years later to hoist the flag of Christianity on the British mainland for the first time, the seeds of Scotland's future were planted.

Jedburgh above, founded by Prince David, later David I, in 1118 is one of Scotland's finest mediaeval buildings, and Castle Kennedy, with its ivy-clad walls right, is noted for its beautiful gardens.

Princes Street, Edinburgh, viewed from the Castle walls overleaf, is one of the world's most famous thoroughfares.

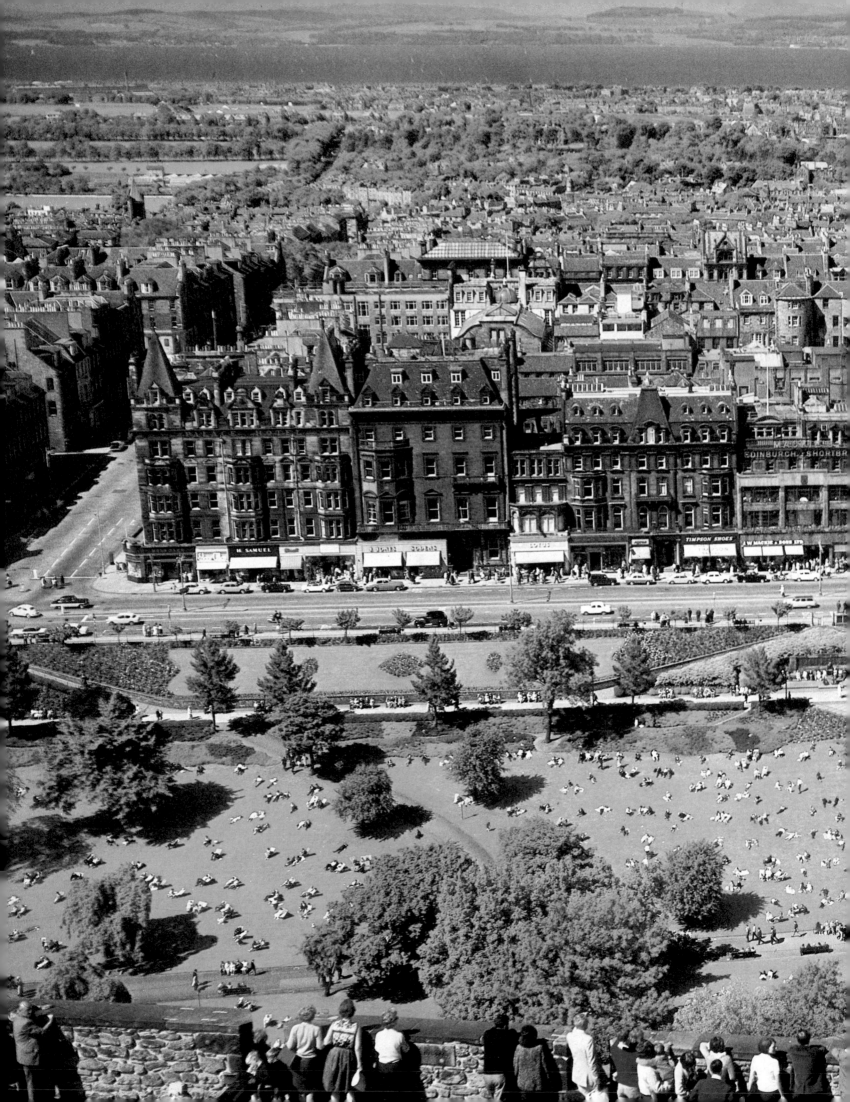

SCOTLAND

St Columba established his monastery on the island of Mull and for more than 30 years, until his death in 597, worked tirelessly to spread the Gospel. In doing so, he was instrumental in forging a unity among the people that would later take the shape of a national identity. Before this could materialise, however, a new threat arrived on Scottish shores: Norse invaders, the most frightening war machine of its time. For more than 200 years the land was decimated by Viking raiders and much of St Columba's work was destroyed. Even the fiercely independent Picts were no match for them. In fact, by the 9th century, the Picts had been all but wiped out, and their territories had gradually fallen under the in-

The cantilevered Forth Railway Bridge above and the Forth Road Bridge right carry road and rail traffic from Edinburgh and the Lowlands. Traditional pipers parade at the Royal Scottish Academy Exhibition left.

SCOTLAND

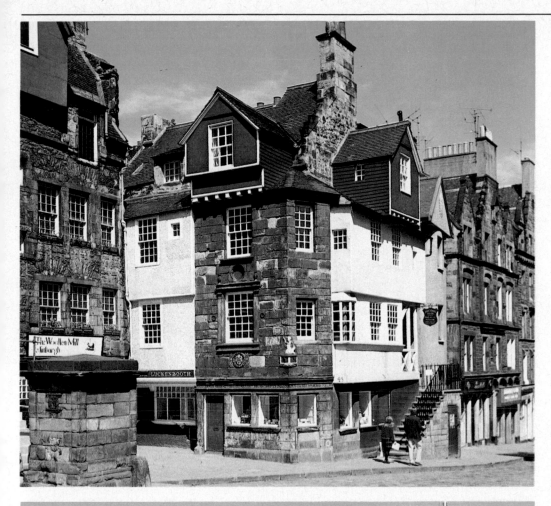

fluence of the Gaelic Kenneth MacAlpine, whose ancestors had come from Ireland.

This period of Scottish history, until the arrival of the Normans from France in the 11th century, is one of its blackest, and represents Scotland's own Dark Ages. The Norman Invasion directly influenced the development of a Scottish character and entity, for rather than adopt Norman ways, many Northern English fled even further north and established themselves in Lowland Scotland. Their language became known for the first time as Scots. Among those refugees was the Anglo-Saxon Princess Margaret, who later married Malcolm III of Scotland, and devoted much of her life to re-establishing the church in Scotland. However, Norman influence could not be resisted and a century later, in the 1300s, French was the official language of Court life, of the clergy and of the nobility south of the Celtic lands (largely the Highlands as we know them today), some of which were still partly occupied by the Norsemen.

Scotland could not consider itself a unified country under one king without the removal of the Norse presence. Then Alexander III grasped the dilemma by the horns. He began to challenge the Norse presence in the Outer Hebrides, and in Orkney and Shetland, angering the Norse King Haakon, who retaliated by ordering an invasion of

Begun by James IV in 1501, the Palace of Holyroodhouse, Edinburgh above is now one of the Queen's residences. John Knox's House in the Royal Mile top left, carefully preserved as a museum, is believed to have been the home of the great Protestant reformer.

261

SCOTLAND

Scotland. Alexander and his troops met Haakon and defeated him at the Battle of Largs, where a peace treaty was finally signed. Alexander was known as the 'peaceable king' and for the next few years Scotland thrived and prospered under his rule.

But peace was shortlived. When Alexander died in 1286, he left no successor, and King Edward I of England saw his chance for a takeover. Using the threat of force, he put his own man, John Balliol, on the Scottish throne. But when Edward called for Scottish support in his campaign against the French, Balliol turned against him. Not only did he refuse the call but, in a bold but foolhardy move, formed an alliance with the French against Edward.

Edward and his army rode into Scotland, bringing death and destruction and ravaging the land. He left behind him a maimed and broken Scotland. He also left with one of the Scot's most treasured national possessions, the Stone of Scone, on which Scottish kings had been crowned. (Sadly enough, the Stone has never been returned to Scotland permanently.) However, a new hero was to give the Scots hope. Robert the Bruce (more French than Scottish – his name was actually Robert de Brus) gained much popular support and eventually had himself crowned king.

With Edward's death in 1307, Robert began to harass the English forces with guerrilla tactics. It was inevitable that there would be an English reaction and it came in 1314, when 20,000 English militiamen massed against a mere 5,000 Scots at a place called Bannockburn. It became an inspiring victory for the outnumbered Scots, who won against enormous odds, but they were unable to turn it into a real political advantage. It was 14 years before they finally reached agreement with the English, but by then too much had happened to destroy any chance of a cordial Anglo-Scots alliance.

Ayr, an attractive resort with a fine fishing harbour right, and Girvan, a popular trout fishing resort above right, are situated along the sheltered Ayrshire coastline, in an area closely associated with Scotland's national poet, Robert Burns, who drew much of his inspiration from the Ayrshire landscape.

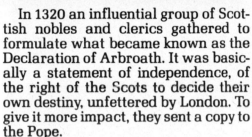

In 1320 an influential group of Scottish nobles and clerics gathered to formulate what became known as the Declaration of Arbroath. It was basically a statement of independence, of the right of the Scots to decide their own destiny, unfettered by London. To give it more impact, they sent a copy to the Pope.

The French Connection

In 1326, building on ties that John Balliol had forged with the French, the 'Auld Alliance' between France and Scotland was formally established. It lasted for centuries, and through it, Scots fought beside Joan of Arc, lined up with the French in the Hundred Years War against the English, and sought refuge in France from English oppression. So close was the relationship that at times it was said: *'He that will France win, must with Scotland first begin'*. These developments could have only one possible effect: to drive a wedge between the English and the Scots. It has not entirely disappeared even today.

Separating Bute from the mainland as it nestles at the foot of the hilly Cowal peninsula, is the beautiful stretch of water known as the Kyles of Bute, pictured right as the P.S. Waverley top right cruises in its calm waters. Also in an area of great natural beauty, the Crinan Canal centre right connects Loch Fyne and the Firth of Clyde with the Western Isles.

SCOTLAND

After Robert the Bruce, and the brief reign of the ineffectual David II, Bruce's grandson became king. Known as Robert the Steward, his accession to the throne signalled the revival of a national identity, and the country flourished. It also had another significance: it was the start of the royal line that was to play such an important role in the affairs of Scotland – the Stuarts.

The fifteenth century saw a buoyant Scotland. Trade and commerce expanded, many monasteries were built and three universities – more than existed in England at the time – were established: St. Andrews (1412), Glasgow (1451) and Aberdeen (1495). But

Standing on land that was once an island, romantic Kilchurn Castle right, begun by Colin Campbell, founder of the Breadalbane family who erected the keep in 1440, occupies a picturesque position beside upper Loch Awe in Strathclyde.

Glasgow in Clydeside, Scotland's most populous city and an important seaport, has been long noted for its outstanding shipbuilding industry. Nightfall brings an unaccustomed softness to the harsh industrial outline of the city's quays and wharves that line the Clyde beyond Kingston Bridge below. A fine example of Victorian architecture, the Town Hall left stands at the heart of Paisley.

fortune did not smile in the same way on the monarchy. After Robert, James I was assassinated in 1437, James II, whose reign began when he was six, was killed accidentally by an exploding cannon, and James III, who came to the throne at the age of nine, was also the victim of assassination.

With James IV, hopes rose once more. Quarrels with England seemed to have been patched up and the future relationship between the two countries assured when James married Margaret Tudor, sister of Henry VIII. But James, an impetuous extrovert, quarrelled with Henry (not the easiest of men to deal with) and while his brother-in-law was away fighting the French, James launched an invasion of England. But it was ill-conceived and badly prepared. It ended in a major defeat for James at Flodden in 1513. All that had been gained at Bannockburn, almost exactly two centuries earlier, was lost in a moment of folly and stupidity.

James V succeeded to the throne and cemented Scotland's continuing relationship with France, marrying, first, the daughter of Francis I of France

A huge Cross of Lorraine on Lyle Hill left, above the important industrial and ship-building town of Greenock, commemorates Free French sailors who died in the Battle of the Atlantic during the Second World War. Robert Burns was born at Alloway, only two miles south of Ayr, and a statue above stands outside Ayr station as a tribute to the famous bard with whom the town is specially linked.

SCOTLAND

and after her death, Mary of Guise. The latter bore him a child (whom James survived by only a few hours), a daughter who was to become perhaps one of the most tragic figures of history – the future Mary Queen of Scots.

While her mother ruled Scotland as Regent, Mary spent most of her childhood in France, was raised as a Catholic and married the French Dauphin. In 1561, a widow, she returned to Scotland to succeed her mother. But Scotland wasn't ready for Mary. Under the stern, puritanical influence of the Calvinist John Knox, the Scottish parliament had recently denounced Catholicism as extreme and corrupt, and had proclaimed Protestantism as Scotland's faith. Now they were faced with a Catholic monarch who further angered her subjects by marrying twice more; first to Darnley (murdered in 1567), then to Boswell. Opposition grew too much for her and she fled to

London, where Elizabeth regarded her as a threat to the English throne and had her imprisoned in the Tower of London. She was beheaded in Fotheringay Castle.

James VI, the son of her marriage to Darnley, succeeded to the Scottish throne. He had two distinct advantages – he was Protestant and also heir to the English throne, which he inherited on Elizabeth's death in 1603. He became James I of England, and James VI of Scotland. And so, the stage was finally set for a rapport between the English and the Scots. But it wasn't meant to be. James virtually abandoned Scotland and, when he tried to insist on English-style church services and hymnals in Scottish churches, the

Scots, led by the single-minded Knox, resisted.

The struggle resulted in deadlock, and the whole dispute was put aside when the English found their time occupied with a Civil War between the Royalists and Cromwell's Parliamentary forces. The wily Scots saw their chance to further their cause by fighting beside Cromwell and helping him win at Marston Moor. For their support in overthrowing Charles I, Cromwell granted the Scots their Covenants — guarantees of the right to worship as they wished.

But then even Cromwell went too far for the Scots. He beheaded Charles I. The Scots reacted by crowning his son, Charles II, on condition that he also guarantee the Covenants. Charles was forced to flee when Cromwell invaded Scotland. But his return was not long delayed, and, on the Protector's death,

The west coast of Scotland abounds in idyllic yachting centres such as Crinan harbour on the Sound of Jura bottom right or Gourock with its picturesque lighthouse far left. Craft of all kinds find moorings in sight of the Paps of Jura top right. Oban, with its attractive harbour above and centre right is a famous West Highland resort in Strathclyde, overlooked by McCaig's Folly, an immense, circular stone structure modelled on the Colosseum in Rome. South of here, Easdale, overlooking the Firth of Lorn left, affords further magnificent sea-scapes and island scenery.

SCOTLAND

Charles inherited the English throne, too. This measure was one of the first steps towards the Act of Union which, in 1707, established Scotland and England as one nation, with one parliament, established Protestantism as the national faith and ended forever any real possibility of a Catholic Stuart's accession to the throne.

This didn't stop the Stuarts from making two determined attempts to overthrow the Act – the Jacobite risings of 1715 and 1745. In 1745, Charles Edward Stuart – Bonnie Prince Charlie – took Perth and Edinburgh, defeated the English at Prestonpans, and with pipes skirling and drums beating, marched as far south as Derby, some 180 miles into England. The English Court was panic-stricken and had even made plans to evacuate London when the Scots suddenly retreated.

The Scots were finally beaten at Culloden by the Duke known as 'The Butcher' of Cumberland. The prince escaped the terrible retribution exacted by the English – the Highland Clearances, disarming of the Clans and banning of the tartan – by fleeing to France, where he died 43 years later. By that time, the Jacobite cause, if not forgotten, had receded far

forgotten, and even now many Scots recall the memory of those days with bitterness.

It may not be an exaggeration to say that the several popular movements for Scottish nationalism since then,

culminating in the heady but temporary parliamentary successes of the 1960s, have roots going back to 1745. Nevertheless, since 1745 Scottish history has been completely intertwined with England's. But what of the

enough into history never again to pose a threat to England or the new, emerging Anglo-Scots relationship. But the unnecessarily cruel and vindictive nature of the English reaction to the uprising was never

Northern Argyll, Strathclyde, is steeped in mountain grandeur where soaring snow-capped peaks right rise to breathtaking heights. Its scenic richness encompasses majestic

scenery, seen across the beautiful Glen Orchy above right, and great sea lochs such as Loch Etive with its impressive glen this page, through which flows an isolated river.

SCOTLAND

land that has seen such a bloody history of its own?

City Dwellers

Including its 787 islands, Scotland covers about 30,000 square miles – more than one-third of the total mass of Great Britain. The population is widely scattered, but a third of the people live in just four cities: Glasgow (about a million), Edinburgh (half a million), Aberdeen and Dundee (about 200,000 each).

Scotland is traditionally divided into the Highlands and Lowlands, both historically and topographically. The

Highlands are the part of the country originally occupied by the Celts. The dividing line between the two sections runs from the north-west corner of Caithness to the south-west border of Scotland, around the Firth of Clyde.

The islands are: The Inner Hebrides (of which Skye is the best known); the Outer Hebrides (including Harris and Lewis); Orkney, Shetland, and the islands of the Firth of Clyde (Arran and others); and of the Firth of Forth (among them Bass Rock). Most of them are inhabited only by sea birds. Less

Dramatically outlined against a misty sunset, Castle Stalker, Appin right stands on an islet in Loch Laich. Not far from Killin, the River Dochart tumbles through a series of falls above, while to the west of the town, nestling at the foot of verdant hills, lies the picturesque community of Tyndrum above right.

than 150 are home to man.

Glasgow is Scotland's oldest city — there was a settlement at a ford over the River Clyde as far back as AD 500. In the 17th and 18th centuries it was a wealthy market town, and its architecture was widely praised throughout Europe. The Clyde had not been dredged into the major waterway it is today and was still, in the words of Moray MacLaren, '...a lowland salmon stream. Around the city by the ford were rich gardens...and fruitful farms' (Shell Guide to Scotland, Ebury 1965). Now, of course, it is a major

Killin above is a popular resort offering among other attractions ideal waters for fishing. Rebuilt in 1745 beside the blue waters of Loch Fyne, Inveraray Castle left, seat of the Dukes of Argyll, has been the headquarters of the Clan Campbell for nearly six centuries.

SCOTLAND

industrial city and seaport. Its size and power are largely the result of a dynamism generated all over Britain during the Victorian era.

The elegant university, a landmark at the top of Gilmorehill, is evidence of this. Built in the 1870s by Sir George Gilbert Scott, it looks dreamily over the western rooftops of the city. The cathedral, which stands on the site of a chapel built by St. Mungo in AD 500, is the only surviving pre-Reformation Gothic structure on the Scottish mainland. The vaulted crypt is one of the best of its kind anywhere in Europe, and the well, in which St Mungo is said to have performed baptisms, still attracts visitors.

The oldest house in Glasgow stands in Cathedral Square. Provand's Lordship, built in the 1470s, is now a museum. The centre of the city is usually accepted to be George Square. It's a gathering place for pigeons, earning for the Square and surrounding streets the nickname, 'Dodge City'. Along with Catholicism and Protestantism, soccer is a major religion in Glasgow. Hampden Park stadium, with a capacity of nearly 150,000, is one of Europe's largest. There are two dates in the Scottish soccer calendar when all three religions come together, the

days when Glasgow Celtic meet Glasgow Rangers. Celtic fans are predominantly Catholic, Rangers mainly Protestant, and although there have been occasional ugly clashes, peace is by and large maintained.

For a long time, a favourite Glasgow pastime has been to take a trip 'doon the watter'. A Clyde steamer from the heart of the city sails past the great Clydeside shipyards and out into the broad waters of the Firth of Clyde. It's worth the trip to see Ailsa Craig, a 1,000-foot rock rising from the water ten miles off the mainland. The city is within easy reach of beautiful countryside. Loch Lomond, for instance, the largest enclosed lake in Britain, and nearby Ben Lomond, a mountain which offers some superb views from its 3,200-foot summit, an easy and worthwhile climb. To the north-east lie the beautiful wooded hills of the Trossachs, immortalised by Scott in his famous poem, *The Lady of the Lake*, and also by Nathaniel Hawthorne in his *English Notebooks*.

Balquhidder on majestic Loch Voil right is best known as the burial place of Robert MacGregor, 'Rob Roy', who died in 1734.

Stirling is dominated by its imposing castle above right which, perched on a 250-foot rock overlooking the battlefield of Bannockburn, was a royal Scottish palace until 1603, when James VI became King of England. Equally formidable, the ruins above are those of Castle Campbell, a stronghold burnt by Cromwell in the 17th century.

Tree-studded Loch Ard, in the lovely Central area, south-east of Ben Lomond top, is an ideal haunt for artists in search of unspoilt beauty. Pictured left is Callander, a popular resort and touring centre for the Trossachs at the confluence of the rivers Teith and Leny, and above in its gentle pastoral setting, the renowned Inveraray Castle.

SCOTLAND

In the direction of the Grampian Mountains, the Braes of Balquhidder provide some of Britain's best camping country. It was here that the legendary Rob Roy MacGregor led the English a merry chase before the 1715 uprising. He is buried near the ruined church of Kirkton.

The Pass of Killiecrankie is a delightful setting for a walk along the banks of the River Garry as it winds through wooded country. There was a battle between the English and Jacobite forces in 1689 near Killiecrankie. A

Pittenweem, with its delightful white-washed cottages far right, quiet harbour right and fishing fleet left perches on the rocky coast of East Neuk in Fife – home of Scotland's kings from Malcolm III until the Union of the Crowns. Amid the charming, cobbled streets of Culross, Fife, lined with 16th and 17th-century red-tiled houses, stand the 'Study' and Cross below, excellently maintained by the National Trust for Scotland.

defeated soldier running from it jumped an unbelievable distance over the river to escape. The spot is now called 'Soldier's Leap'. Just up the road is Pitlochry, a major vacation resort where there are excellent facilities for such sports as pony-trekking, riding, skiing and golf. Blair Castle, a few

miles away, is the seat of the Duke of Atholl. It is famous as the last castle in Britain to withstand a siege – the one mounted by the Jacobites in 1745. It was rebuilt in 1789 as it stands today, and parts of it are open for viewing.

Travellers through the Grampians are rewarded by superb scenery at places like the Devil's Elbow on the Cairnwell Pass, the highest main road in Britain. This is skiing country and over the past ten years, ski and après-ski facilities have been greatly improved. Glenshee and Aviemore in the Cairngorms, offer a huge variety of winter sports facilities such as indoor ski schools, curling rinks, skating, tobogganing and – in summer – pony trekking, rock climbing and sail boarding.

Between the Grampians and the Cairngorms – the highest mountain range in Britain, with several peaks second only to Ben Nevis – lie Braemar and Balmoral on Deeside.

Royal Scotland

Braemar is probably best known today for its celebrated Highland Gatherings, but in 1715 it was where James Edward Stuart first raised the Jacobite banner to herald the Stuart uprising.

The Highland Games have been held at Braemar since 1832, and since Queen Victoria graced them with her

SCOTLAND

presence in 1848 the games have enjoyed royal patronage. The Games consist of piping competitions, tugs-of-war, highland wrestling and dancing, and tossing the caber (which should, according to some experts, be pronounced 'cabber'). The word caber means a branch from a tree. In early days it was literally that, with side shoots and leaves removed for the event. There is no standard size, and the point of the event is to throw the caber end-over-end. Every competitor at the Games must wear a kilt, whether or not he is Scots. Indeed, many competitors these days are not Scots but they still follow the rule and wear a kilt, although not always with precision. Several other towns – Ballater, Aboyne and Oban among them – also stage Highland Games, but the Braemar event, held every September, is the most prestigious.

The castle at Balmoral is the private residence of the Queen. Prince Albert bought it for Queen Victoria in 1852, paying the princely sum of £31,500 for it. He had it re-modelled with granite quarried right on the 24,000-acre Balmoral Estate. The castle is beautifully situated by the Dee, and although glimpses of it can be caught from the road it is sufficiently secluded to afford the Royal Family its necessary privacy. The nearest village to the castle is Crathie, and it is to the kirk there that the Royal Family goes to worship when at Balmoral. In the churchyard is a memorial erected by Queen Victoria as a tribute to her faithful ghillie, John Brown. His house is across the Dee and can be seen from the kirk.

The road to Tomintoul – the highest Highland town – winds through the sometimes forbidding Pass of Ballater, extremely narrow in places, and frequently blocked by winter snows. Eventually it wanders into Tomintoul, centred around a village green. The nearby valley of the Avon (pronounced 'A'an') is regarded by many as one of Scotland's most beautiful glens.

North of Tomintoul is Speyside, one of the major whisky distilling areas, with Dufftown at its centre. Rome was built on seven hills, so the local saying goes, but Dufftown stands on seven stills. There is more lore and legend connected with whisky than any other Scottish institution. It has its own mystique which canny Scots are careful to perpetuate, with the result that the drink is one of Scotland's

Standing between the meadows of the North and South Inch at the head of the River Tay estuary, the 'Fair City' of Perth above and bottom right was Scotland's capital for a century until 1437. South-west of the city lie the world-famous Gleneagles golf courses top right. It is Fife, however, which is regarded as the home of golf. Founded in 1754, the Royal and Ancient Golf Club of St Andrews, with its Road Hole, the seventeenth, on the Old Course shown centre right, is the foremost in the world.

The now-ruined cathedral in the university city of St Andrews left was founded in 1160.

major exports. The first record of whisky appears in 1494, but authorities agree it was probably drunk long before that. It is defined as 'a spirit obtained by distillation from a mash of cereal grains turned into sugar by the fermentation of malt.' There have been many second-rate imitations, but the real thing is in a class by itself. Robbie Burns took it with water, sugar and lemon; Queen Victoria topped her port with it; the purists drink it neat, or with a dash of loch water, but never, never with ice!

A detour towards Aberdeen brings you to the delightful Craigievar Castle. It was built in 1626 and, remarkably, can be seen today almost exactly as it was then. Nothing has been added or changed. In fact, it comes complete with its own ghost, reputedly that of a former owner who was forced at sword point to jump to his death from a window.

SCOTLAND

The most beautiful approach to Aberdeen is by the coast road. *'The one haunting and exasperatingly lovable city in Scotland'*, as it has been called, stretches elegantly between the Rivers Don and Dee. It is also known as the Granite City, much of it built from local granite mined at Rubislaw, which at 465 feet is the world's deepest quarry. Quarrying has been one of the city's major industries for many years, and Aberdeen granite is found all over the world – in pavements, graveyards, office buildings and other places where solid permanence is needed. But oil is king in Aberdeen today, and you are reminded of its presence under the grey waters of the North Sea by the trappings of the industry visible from virtually every street corner. Plush oil company buildings, fleets of tankers, survey offices and a new crop of leisure centres, bars and restaurants provide oilmen with plenty of ways to spend their money.

Although declining, the fishing industry is still a major employer in Aberdeen, and the daily early morning fish market is a reminder of the city's heritage and is well worth a visit.

Local history is preserved in the Provost Skene's House, the oldest part of which dates from 1545. Within the city the Aulton, or old town, of Aberdeen, belongs for the most part to the University. It has become a stylish mixture of the best of the old with tasteful new student buildings.

From Aberdeen, the search for Scotland continues round the coast through Fraserburgh, with its famous lifeboat station, and Banff, an ancient fishing town, and a stop well worth making at Fochabers. Here, at the end of the 18th century, the fourth Duke of Gordon decided to greatly extend his castle. Trouble was, the village was in the way – so he demolished it. But he commissioned an entirely new village that today stands as a fine example of Georgian planning and architecture. Ironically, little remains of the old castle that brought about such sweep-

Tayside's magnificent wooded scenery and turquoise lochs include Loch Tummel seen from Queen's View left; the westward vista of snow-capped Schiehallion beyond Loch Rannoch above left; and dazzling Loch Faskally, east of Loch Rannoch above right. From the Hermitage Bridge close by the cathedral town of Dunkeld can be seen the cascading Falls of Bran right.

ing change.

Elgin, with the remains of a fine 13th century cathedral, lies about ten miles to the west. A few miles inland is Pluscarden Abbey, a monastery that dates back to 1230. For many years its monks have welcomed visitors and delighted in showing them around their early English church.

Butcher's Battlefield

The road runs north through Forres, where Shakespeare set the 'blasted heath' of *Macbeth* fame, and on towards Culloden, the burial ground of Jacobite hopes in 1746. A memorial stone mound marks the site where the English forces, under William, Duke of Cumberland, took just 40 minutes to rout the Stuart rebels. During this brief battle, Cumberland undoubtedly committed unnecessary acts of brutality, but he returned to great acclaim in London, where the flower 'Sweet William' was named after him. To Scots, however, the flower has always been known as 'Stinking Willy'.

SCOTLAND

Skirting Inverness, and running south-west, are the menacing waters of Loch Ness, in some places 750 feet deep. What lurks in those depths? No one knows, but one thing is certain: as long as people want to believe in the existence of a monster the gloomy loch will continue to interest them. If the monster's existence is ever disproved, Loch Ness might fall into comparative obscurity. Inverness, *'the gateway to the Highlands'*, is also considered the Highland capital, housing many administrative offices for such Highland activities as forestry, deer hunting and small farming. Urquhart Castle, overlooking the western shore of Loch Ness, has been a ruin for nearly 300 years and much of what now remains dates from 1509. There are two unopened vaults. It is said that one contains treasure, the other plague-infested clothing. But no one knows which is which and, not surprisingly, no one has ever tried to find out.

On through Drumnadrochit and Cannich to Beauly. Not far away is Beaufort Castle, the seat of the Lovat family, once ardent Jacobites. The ruins of the original castle, which was destroyed by Cumberland in one of his purges, can be seen in a terraced

A number of beautiful old buildings dot the Grampian landscape, among them, the turreted Midmar right, Braemar overlooking the Dee above, and the ruined Elgin Cathedral above left.

Lying one mile north-east of Cruden Bay is the Bullers of Buchan left, a 200 foot chasm in the craggy cliffs that jut out into the North Sea.

SCOTLAND

garden of the present castle, itself a fine example of Victorian styling.

Between the Firths of Beauly and Cromarty lies the Black Isle; not an island, but a peninsula. It is so-called because of its rich farmland. Snow rarely seems to settle for long on the black soil. In one of its villages, Fortrose, the remains of an ancient cathedral date back to the time of David I.

Dingwall, the county town of Ross and Cromarty, was for many years a Norse town and the name comes from the Norse word 'thing', meaning parliament. It is dominated by a tower on the hill overlooking the town, a memorial to General Sir Hector MacDonald. He began life as a clothmaker's assistant in Dingwall, joined the army, was decorated for bravery and rose through the ranks, eventually earning a knighthood. But allegations of homosexuality were made against him (which at the turn of the last century could surely ruin a career in the British Army) and in 1903 he took his own life. To his home town of Dingwall, however, he remains a dashing hero.

Further north, past Invergordon, where a section of the Royal Navy mutinied in 1931, is the attractive ancient Royal Burgh of Tain. As the birthplace of St Duthac, it has been a site of pilgrimages for many years. It is also where the wife, sister and daughter of Robert the Bruce were betrayed to their English pursuers. The Collegiate Church there dates back to the 14th century, and there is an interesting prison, housing a curfew bell, presumably used by the English to enforce regulations at the time of the Highland Clearances.

The original structure at Bonar Bridge, over the Dornoch Firth, was designed in 1811 by Thomas Telford, one of England's great engineers, after the Meikle Ferry disaster in which 100 people were drowned.

Dornoch, the county town of Sutherland is, according to Michael Brander, *'a mediaeval town and on top of that a mediaeval cathedral town...something of a surprise.'* (*Around the Highlands*, Bles 1967). The cathedral is now the parish church and contains an unusual organ presented to the church in 1907 by the Scottish-American philanthropist, Andrew Carnegie. Dornoch is perhaps best known for its splendid golf course, which attracts visitors from all over the world. St Andrews is, of course, the number one Scottish

The Royal Burgh of Aberdeen these pages is the third largest city in Scotland and the country's largest fishing port. It is also a noted university and cathedral centre. Lying on the estuaries of the Rivers Dee and Don, in addition to being Northern Scotland's leading commercial centre, its major industries including not only fishing but also engineering, shipbuilding, paper making, granite and chemicals, the city also attracts many summer visitors as one of the country's coastal resorts. It is also renowned for outstandingly beautiful parks and gardens.

SCOTLAND

course, and is also the golf capital of the world, regularly holding tournaments that attract the best international players. Its ancient cathedral, castle and university are 'musts' for any visit to Scotland. Dornoch also has the distinction of having witnessed the last execution of a witch in Scotland. According to Moray McLaren, *'Janet Horn was tarred, feathered and roasted, accused of having turned her daughter into a pony and having her shod by the devil.'* A stone marks the spot where this unfortunate woman met such a terrible fate.

Gothic Mistake

Further up the coast lies Golspie, a fishing village and small resort town within easy reach of the beautiful Dunrobin Glen. And a mile to the north is the strangely-designed Dunrobin Castle, seat of the Dukes of Sutherland. The present building which, says Michael Brander, appears to be *'all minarets and turrets, a Gothic mistake'*, is mainly 19th century. Its contents, rather than the structure itself, are the chief attraction. Part of the castle is open as a museum, housing a collection of mementos gathered by the family through generations, both at home and abroad. It also contains a fine representation of much of the wildlife found in Scotland, such as polecat, otter, wildcat, pine-marten, badger, fox, stoat and weasel, and most of the exhibition cases bear personal labels written, presumably, by the family member contributing the exhibit.

Wick lies on the coast road to John o' Groats and, like Dingwall, there is evidence of its Norse ancestry. The name comes from the Norse for 'bay'. The Old Man of Wick, today just a square stone tower, was in its heyday an impregnable castle perched on rocks overlooking the sea, and was probably built by the Norsemen. It's a bustling town with a market and an airport serving the major Scottish cities as well as Orkney to the north-east.

In nearby Sinclair Bay are the ruins

Macduff above left is an important herring-fishing town in Banff Bay. Autumnal tints right, eclipsed by the advent of winter above right, bring a touch of magic to Loch Moy, while mystery of a different kind prevails in the depths of Loch Ness left, overlooked by Urquhart Castle overleaf.

SCOTLAND

Misty sunsets in frosted winter landscapes, over wooded Loch Laggan *left and below left* and Loch Ness *far left,* enhance the drama of the Highland scenery.

A magnificent piece of 19th-century engineering, the Caledonian Canal *below,* begun by Thomas Telford in 1803 and opened forty-four years later, once provided a safe alternative passage to the stormy route round Cape Wrath. Made obsolete by the coming of large steamships, today this unique canal is mainly used by pleasure craft and fishing boats.

of the neighbouring castles of Sinclair and Girnigoe. In the latter, the fourth Earl of Caithness, believing his son was plotting against him, imprisoned the young man in the dungeons for seven years, until he died of 'famine and vermin'.

John o' Groats is called the most northerly point of Britain. However, it is not. That distinction belongs to Dunnett Head, to the west. John o' Groats itself is little more than a sprinkle of white-washed cottages, a hotel, some shops (including the inevitable souvenir stores) and a signpost pointing south that bears the legend 'Land's End – 874 miles'. This, perhaps more than anything, sums up the size of Britain for the American visitor. The distance from one end of the British Isles to the other is about as far as the distance from Los Angeles to Portland, or from New York to St Louis.

John o' Groats is named after a Dutchman, one of three brothers who ran the ferry to Orkney in the 16th century. According to the story, when they and their families numbered eight, a disagreement broke out over who was in charge. The only solution was to

289

SCOTLAND

build an octagonal house with eight doors so that each member of the family could enter by his or her own door and sit at the octagonal table inside without taking precedence over any other. Sadly, the house has long since disappeared.

Between John o' Groats and Dunnett Head, and barely visible from the road, is the Castle of Mey, built in 1567 and now the private retreat of Queen Elizabeth the Queen Mother. From Dunnett Head, with its fine sweep of sand, can be seen the Islands of Orkney. There are 67 in all, of which about 20 are inhabited. Mainland is the largest. Its capital, Kirkwall, is 900 years old, with roots in the Norse tradition, and has all the appearance of a Scandinavian town. Stromness, the other main settlement on the island, is much more Scottish. It was a Celtic fishing village until mainland Scots started using it as a port for trade in the 17th century. Hudson Bay Company vessels used to call there regularly too. Now it is content, and quieter, as a small local fishing community.

The second largest Orkney island is Hoy, with a range of spectacular rocky peaks that makes it superb climbing country. The most challenging to the climber is the Old Man of Hoy, a vertical column of basalt rising 450 feet straight up from the western edge of the island. It has been scaled by only the most accomplished of climbers. There is plenty for the historically inclined on Hoy, including an Early Bronze Age tomb known as the Dwarfie Stone. Indeed, nearly all the Orkney Islands are rich in prehistoric artifacts. The Islanders are mainly farmers, and the fishing industry is rare, although visitors find the inland lochs abundant in brown trout.

The Shetland Isles are 60 miles north-east of Orkney. Once you get beyond Unst, the most northerly of them, there is nothing but endless ocean between you and the North Pole. There are about 100 islands in the Shetlands, some 20 of which are inhabited. Mainland is the largest, with Lerwick, its capital, a maze of narrow streets. It is a cosmopolitan

Ben Nevis, at 4,406 feet Britain's highest mountain, seen from the Caledonian Canal right and above far right, from Banavie below far right and from the Highland village of Tulloch below centre right, dominates Fort William at its base above right.

SCOTLAND

town, often host to foreign fishing crews from Russia and Japan, as well as western Europe. The North Sea oil boom has brought to Lerwick, as it has to Orkney, the personnel and paraphernalia of oil exploration.

One festival with indelible Viking links takes place in Lerwick each January. This is Up-Helly-Aa, an advance welcome to the arrival of the summer sun following the short days and long darkness of winter. Unlike Orkney, Shetland is mainly a fishing community, but it is also the home of the world famous Shetland ponies, bred on the 25-square-mile island of Fetlar. Shetland wool is also a major industry for the islands.

Part of the British Isles, Shetland, nevertheless, is nearer the Arctic Circle than it is to London. Its remote-

ness from the British capital was a problem for a Shetlander sending his army draft papers during the last World War. He was asked to enter the name of his nearest railway station. He thought hard for a moment then wrote – quite accurately – 'Bergen, Norway'. And at that time it was occupied by the Germans!

Back on the mainland, and continuing west along the north shore of Caithness, the stark whiteness of the atomic energy reactor at Dounreay appears on the landscape. Opened in 1960, it was one of Britain's first atomic reactors, a herald of the new nuclear age.

Highland Sport

But just a few miles south, on the moors of Caithness around Altna-

In the Great Glen of the Highlands lie Loch Unagin below left and Loch Oich left, the highest of the chain of lochs linked by the Caledonian Canal.

Bagpipes far left resound through the mountains overhanging Glencoe, the Glen of Weeping which, in 1692, was the scene of a terrible massacre. In that year soldiers led by Robert Campbell of Glen Lyon slaughtered forty Macdonalds and MacIan, the chief, in memory of whom the monument below was erected near the entrance to the glen.

A crisp blanket of snow covers the banks of Loch Leven right and a glowing sunset envelops the cliffs of the Isle of Mull below right.

breac, lies country that for years has provided the field and stream sports of Scotland, a real slice of the country's heritage: hunting, shooting and fishing, Scottish style.

The Thurso river provides excellent salmon fishing, there are many hill lochs for trout, and on the moors, grouse shooting, deer hunting and falconry. Grouse are peculiarly Scottish: the Red, found on higher ground, and the Black (the male in fact is ebony and purple with a splash of crimson on his head), near woodland. They are protected for much of the year, but the Glorious Twelfth – of August – heralds the new shooting season, and many of England's leading restaurants go to

SCOTLAND

elaborate lengths to serve the first grouse of the year.

In recent years, Scottish field sports have brought wealthy men from around the world to sample the very special delights of the Scottish moor, once the preserve of the Highlander himself, then of the English aristocracy. There is little to compare with a sparkling day in search of deer, with a knowledgeable local Scot charting the terrain. It is said that the best way to end such a day is to sit down to a meal of venison, cooked by the wife of the head stalker who made the kill.

Across the northern stub of Scotland, heading for the west coast, lies the beautiful, unspoiled Strath Naver, its peace and tranquillity belying its stormy history, when small farmers and their families were forcibly evicted from the fertile land in the infamous Highland Clearances. At the southern end of the valley lies Loch Naver in a bowl in the hills. On its northern bank are two rundown, but preserved, 19th century farming townships, Grummore and Grumbeg. Loch Eriboll lies to the west, a sea loch with a depth of up to 150 feet that makes it a superb natural harbour. About six miles along the coast towards Cape Wrath is the remarkable Smoo Cave. Actually three caves, its largest is 200 feet long and about 120 high. An 80-foot waterfall plunges into the second cave.

The aptly named Cape Wrath is well known to sailors. Its rugged cliff face rising 400 feet out of the sea, with dangerous reefs below, can be seen from nearly 30 miles. A lighthouse beams out a warning message to seamen. The road down to the glorious scenery of Suilven leads past the ruins of Ardvreck Castle standing on the shores of Loch Assynt. At nearly 2,400 feet, Suilven is far from the highest mountain in Britain but its strange conical shape rising from the dense Glen Canisp Forest, its renown as a mountaineers' and geologists' paradise,

Glencoe is the scene of brooding, precipitous elevations such as the Three Sisters at its head right and the twin Buchaille Etive peaks overshadowing the climber's hut below left. At the entrance to the glen rises the Pap of Glencoe below and through the awe-inspiring pass below right and bottom left winds the cascading Glencoe River bottom and overleaf.

SCOTLAND

make it one of the most remarkable. Its upper slopes are also abundant in eagle, falcon and buzzard and, lower down, ptarmigan. To the south lies Ullapool, now a fishing village and tourist centre, but once a major port for the Scots emigrating by the thousand to North America at the time of the Clearances.

In some parts around Ullapool live strict sects from within the Free Kirk of Scotland who on Sundays, for instance, remove their tourist bed and breakfast signs, do no washing, and refuse to buy (or sell if they are shopkeepers) milk, food, newspapers, gas and so on. Religion is taken very seriously in these parts: witness the story of a visitor attending morning service in a strict Free Kirk, and joining in lustily with the hymns and responses. The regular congregation, favouring a much more discreet demeanour, grew

increasingly annoyed. Finally, one of them complained. *'But I'm praising the Lord'*, the visitor explained. *'Sir,'* said an old churchgoer, *'in this church we do not praise anything'*.

Among the most popular attractions on the west coast are the tropical gardens of Inverewe, thriving in the mild, damp climate of Wester Ross, close to the warming Gulf Stream and enjoying more than 60 inches of rain a year. At any time the gardens are lush with vegetation, and imported plants such as Monterey Pines, eucalyptus, and Australian tree ferns grow just as happily as they do in their native soils. Loch Maree, running south from Gairloch, is one of the most beautiful, the country's first nature reserve, fringed by Ben Eighe, and the majestic Torridon mountain range, and overlooked by the brooding peak of Slioch to the north. Strome Ferry, on Loch Carron,

used to be the departure point for the Isle of Skye and the Hebrides; nowadays the Kyle of Lochalsh has taken over in these parts.

Skye, the most northerly of the Inner Hebrides and the largest of the Western Isles, has its own lore and legend and a very distinct personality of its own. Watching the sun setting over the Outer Hebrides islands of Harris and Lewis from Skye is an unforgettable experience. Just 50 miles long, with the mysterious Cuillin Hills in the south, the Island seems to have a permanent bluish light of its own, except on those very rare, perfectly clear days. It is mountainous throughout, with the Trotternish range in the north, where you can see the vertical stack of rock called the Old Man of Storr, and the strange rock formation of the Quiraing. Dunvegan Castle, dating from the ninth century, is the seat of the Macleod Clan, and is also a major attraction on the Island.

A few miles to the south lies the Island of Rum, now largely a centre for the study of the large Red Deer population and, consequently, not always accessible to the traveller. To the east of Rum lies Eig (pronounced 'egg'), a 24-square-mile paradise for the botanist and naturalist. A wide range of plant life flourishes there as well as several species of animal life peculiar to the island.

The remaining islands of the larger Inner Hebrides are Raasay, where Johnson and Boswell stopped on their celebrated Highland tour; Rona, which is virtually uninhabited, lies between Skye and the mainland; and the islands of Muck, Jora, Islay, Coll, Tiree, Colonsay and Canna.

Anglers' Delights

To the north-west are the Outer Hebrides, consisting of Barra, Eriskay, South and North Uist, Benbecula, Harris and Lewis. The 1,500 inhabitants of Barra live by farming and fishing and are not reliant on tourists. Three-mile-

Mallaig right is a large herring port on the rocky shores of North Morar.

Overlooking majestic Loch Shiel, stands the monument at Glenfinnan overleaf, and west of the monument, beautiful Loch Eilt left is set in the wild scenery of this heavily indented Atlantic edge of Scotland. To the east lie the undisturbed waters of Loch Eil above right.

long Eriskay is where Bonnie Prince Charlie first landed from France in 1745, and it retains much lore and legend from that time, with an especially fine heritage of folk songs.

South Uist has a population of about 2,000 (largely farmers), and a tradition of producing the finest pipers. It is only 22 miles long but packed into that length are no less than 190 freshwater lochs – a delight for trout fishermen. It was on South Uist, just a few months after setting foot on Eriskay, that Bonnie Prince Charlie sought refuge after the battle of Culloden and from where he was rescued by Flora MacDonald. North Uist is much more Norse in character and exclusively Protestant, in contrast to Catholic South Uist. It has many standing stone monuments and, a rare claim in the Hebrides, abundant numbers of salmon and trout. However, the island

SCOTLAND

of Benbecula, probably the flattest of the Outer Hebrides group, is also an angler's dream.

Harris and Lewis are actually connected although they are described as islands. However, they are intrinsically different. Harris is mountainous, rocky and almost exclusively a fishing community where both the English and Gaelic spoken are, to the discerning ear, different from that spoken on Lewis which lies just 30 feet away across a small connecting bridge.

Lewis is larger, flatter and less appealing scenically but Moray McLaren has no doubt that *'even among the highly individual Celtic community, the Lewis folk are remarkable . . . exhilarating.'*

Back on the mainland, and heading south from Strome Ferry, the road leads past the romantically-situated Eilean Donnan Castle, one of the most

Overlooking Loch Duich, the Five Sisters of Kintail highlight the east end of Glen Shiel below right.

Eilean Donnan Castle left, above and right, built in 1220 by Alexander II of Scotland, is now a museum and clan war memorial.

photographed of all Scottish castles. It stands on a promontory of Loch Duich and overlooks the point where Lochs Alsh and Long join Duich. At the head of Loch Duich are the peaks known as the Five Sisters of Kintail, each over 3,000 feet high, and just to the north is one of Britain's highest and most picturesque waterfalls – the Falls of Glomach, about 750 feet from top to bottom.

Ben Nevis rises 4,406 feet, but with its rounded top lacks the impact of lesser peaks. It can be comfortably climbed by the more active tourist on the gentle slopes from Achintee, a round trek that takes about eight hours. But on the other side, the northeast face offers even experienced climbers a real challenge.

The road to Spean Bridge provides spectacular views of Aonach Mor (4,000 feet) and the great corries of Ben Nevis. Spean Bridge was the site of one of the first battles in the 1745 Uprising, and was also a commando-training centre during World War II.

Glen Roy – a geological curiosity – starts near here. The Parallel Roads run through this glacial valley, once a lake, on which time and erosion

SCOTLAND

worked to produce this startling phenomenon.

Glenfinnan, at the head of Loch Shiel on the Road to the Isles, is a beautiful spot – romantic even without its Bonnie Prince Charlie associations, commemorated by a monument: It is where the Young Pretender raised his standard to gather the Clans about him for the march on England.

The Road to the Isles ends at Mallaig where the ubiquitous MacBrayne steamers can be taken for many parts of the Hebrides and for Skye. Mallaig is renowned for its kippers – a form of smoked herring fish. Nearby Loch Morar is the deepest inland waterway in Britain and with depths of up to 1,000 feet is surpassed in Europe by only one other lake. Loch Morar, too, is supposed to have a monster lurking below.

Oban, on the west coast overlooking Mull, is an attractive town of some 3,000 people. Its busy harbour, used by fishing vessels and MacBrayne steamers headed for the Isles, is overlooked by MacCaig's Folly. A circular stadium-like structure, the building was started in the 1890's by a wealthy and eccentric bank manager, MacCaig, who intended it to be a museum. But when he died during the course of its construction his dream died with him.

From Oban, Mull and Iona are within easy reach by steamer. Mull has a great variety of scenery – forest, moorland, hills – and its main town, Tobermory, is a most impressive sight when approached from the sea. Apart from tourism, fishing is now its major industry. Iona, off the south-west of Mull, is famous worldwide. It was to this charming island that St Columba brought Christianity in AD 563. The Abbey, restored around the turn of the century, holds regular services, and visitors from everywhere come to attend them and to see the work of the Iona Community which was founded in 1938 to maintain the old monastery ruins and the burial place of the Scot-

Named after an early Norwegian king, Kyleakin right overlooks the narrow strait of Kyle Akin. Nearby stands Castle Moil top right, for centuries a stronghold of the Mackinnons of Strath.

Ranged along the secluded inlet of Loch Carron, the charming fishing and craft community of Plockton centre right and facing page forms part of the Balmacara estate.

tish kings. The island itself is a delight, seemingly as untouched and unspoiled as when St Columba arrived.

The other side of Loch Awe from Oban is Inverary, the county town of Argyll. It is the seat of the chief of the Campbell Clan, the Duke of Argyll. Inveraray Castle is one of the chief attractions for the visitor to this delightful town, but it has been ravaged by fire throughout the years. In 1877 there was considerable fire damage and almost 100 years later a more widespread blaze broke out, resulting in the loss of many fine works of art and the closing of the castle to the public.

Going up through Glen Croe to Loch Fyne there used to be a steep climb, and at the top of the pass there is still a stone plaque inscribed *'Rest, and be thankful'*. Many a walker of old was pleased to do so. Once through the

pass, Glasgow is almost within sight, and the traveller is again back in the Lowlands.

Edinburgh, only 30 miles east of Glasgow is, according to its inhabitants, a world apart. It has elegance and style. Princes Street compares with anything Europe has to offer, and the 1,000-year-old castle perched high above the town is a delight to the eye. As McLaren says: *'From Edinburgh's highest point you can see half over southern Scotland and into the Highland Hills. Everywhere in the streets you may come upon a corner from which you will catch unexpected glimpses of sea or hills or remote countryside.'* The city developed at the beginning of the 19th century and until the 1850s simply consisted of the buildings of the Old Town grouped around the Castle on the Rock. St Margaret's Chapel, built in 1076 and containing so much of Scotland's history, the Canongate Tolbooth, John Knox's House, the Palace of Holyroodhouse, Parliament House (now the Scottish Law Courts), and the Register House are just a few of the places any serious visitor must include in his itinerary.

In the wild Holyrood Park stands

At the stony head of Loch Inver, the small coastal resort of Lochinver can be seen bottom left, centre left Kinlochbervie on Loch Inchard, top left the noted east coast leisure centre of Wick, and right the leading sea-angling centre of Ullapool. Pictured above right are the rock formations of Muckle and Little Stacks at Duncansby Head, and above imposing Dunbeath Castle, south of Dunbeath.

SCOTLAND

Beyond John O'Groats above, near the extreme north-east tip of the Scottish mainland, lie the Shetland and Orkney islands. Many of the Shetlands are uninhabited but Lerwick with its picturesque harbour above right bustles with boats from many lands and Mid Yell left is a busy Shetland port. Skara Brae right, a remarkable neolithic village settlement, stands on the largest Orkney Island of Mainland.

Arthur's Seat, a superb 822-foot panoramic vista atop a natural hill. The Edinburgh Tattoo, a fine demonstration at the floodlit Castle of military marching by pipe and drum bands, and the Edinburgh Festival, offering much that is best and new in the arts, are two annual events that bring thousands to this most attractive of cities.

Moving down towards the Border Country, Glen Trool Forest, nearly 200 square miles of national park forest, includes the highest peak in the south of Scotland – The Merrick (2,764 feet) – and the curiosity of a loch within a loch. Loch Enoch surrounds an island which itself has a loch – in this case it is technically a lochan. Robert the Bruce's guerrilla forces at Bannockburn defeated an English contingent in Glen Trool. A memorial at the east end

SCOTLAND

of the Loch records the victory.

Border Country is the land of the River Tweed which, for more than ten miles, actually defines the border between England and Scotland. For that reason it has a special place in Scottish hearts. Sir Walter Scott spent the last 20 years of his life at Abbotsford on its banks. Its waters nourish the rich pastures of the area, its salmon and trout are among the finest, and it feeds the prosperous Border towns of Peebles, Melrose and Kelso – where the tweed fabric is produced.

The border itself runs from near Lamberton on the east coast to Gretna Green, where young couples, under age by English law, used to elope to marry under the more lenient laws of Scotland.

Now discreetly marked by simple road signs, the border nevertheless remains to many Scots the most important one they will ever cross. It can be a highly emotional moment, returning to Scotland, as even many non-Scots have found. Though Scots may leave home, Scotland never really leaves their hearts.

IRELAND

IRELAND

Over the years the land of Ireland has become familiar to people throughout the world who have never visited the 'Emerald Isle'. It has featured in dozens of feature films and documentaries and was seen by many millions during the televising of Pope John Paul II's highly successful visit in September 1979. What viewers throughout the world shared on their television screens was the rejoicing of a majority of a disciplined people, and a glimpse was caught of a land of much colour and contrast. The autumn sun shone, and a large fragment of the whole that goes to make up the Irish was witnessed by the viewing world. Although small in geographical and physical terms, this tiny spot on the globe gets its fair share of exposure on television, in the world's press, and on radio. More often than not its current news in relation to one area of the country is sad and violent and bloody, but at all times this small off-shore island of a slightly larger European off-shore island, commands the attention and interest of its many, many millions of relations throughout the world, and notably in Great Britain, in the United States, in Australia, and particularly in emergent African nations where Irish missionaries have laboured and taught for over a century.

There are, for example, one million Irish-born and over three million Irish-related people resident in Great Britain today, in fact, more Irish than there are living in Ireland, and between twenty and thirty millions more Irish born and Irish-related in America. Not all of them know all that much about the country of their ancestors and its roots, and for those with a general interest in the Irish nation, some gathering of the facts, and a bird's-eye view, can help to broaden and deepen the interest in a place and a people which alternatively delights and exasperates the civilised world, but never loses its touch for the romantic or the magical, or its sense of humour or its sense of the absurd, and always

Crossed by many fine bridges, the River Liffey flows through the heart of Dublin left, this fascinating city with its wide streets and spacious squares, that ranks as one of Europe's most eminent capitals.

IRELAND

remains supremely beautiful, and full of colour.

The island of Ireland is, of course, part of the main continent of Europe. It is situated as part of the most north-westerly area of the European land mass between fifty-one and a half degrees and fifty-five and a half degrees latitude north, and five and a half and ten and a half degrees longitude west. Separating Ireland from Great Britain is the Irish Sea, about ten miles at its narrowest, and one hundred and twenty miles at its widest. The land of Ireland comprises 32,595 square miles, and roughly speaking, the greatest length of the country is three hundred and two miles, and at its greatest width it is one hundred and seventy-five miles. No point within the island is more than seventy or eighty miles from the sea-shore.

The Irish Sea to the east is about two hundred metres deep, and is a rough enough sea in the winter, particularly in the more exposed and open south-west. The Atlantic Ocean to the west

Turf cutters above and centre right; the convivial pub interior in Maghery top right, and the farmer and his calf on Rossnowlagh Beach, Donegal Bay right, were photographed in Ireland's most northerly county – Donegal – famed for its magnificent, unspoilt scenery.

Sheep are shown being tagged far right, perhaps to graze, later, on the lovely headland overleaf.

IRELAND

presents an awesome sight at any time of the year, with its sixty-foot rollers and breakers hurling themselves all down the west coast. America is two thousand four hundred miles away to the west.

The entire Irish coastline adds up to over three thousand five hundred miles. Because of its sea-girt nature the land of Ireland enjoys a moderate climate. Winters are relatively mild, and summers reasonably warm, the occasional summer being positively Mediterranean. The months of July and August are the warmest, averaging 15°C or 59°F. May and June are the months with the most sun. Snow and ice, except on high mountains, are rare, but there is always the unexpected and an exceptional winter.

Overall, the moderate influence of the warm Gulf Stream, drifting down the west coast, makes for sub-tropical and unusual foliage and flowers and fauna in the south-west.

From the prevailing winds coming in from the Atlantic Ocean comes the rain, which is heavier in the west, and averages about thirty inches in the east.

Because of its westerly geographical position, there are more hours of daylight in Ireland than in the rest of Europe and a clear sky with light and lucidity which is forever changing, and best described in paintings or visual terms as an 'Expressionist' light. This is the overriding beauty above the landscape. To add to this overall beauty of sky and light, the physical features of Ireland are such that every range of scenery in Europe is available in one small isle. No two county divisions of the country are alike.

Generally speaking, Ireland comprises a central undulating plain of limestone, encircled by a coastal range of highland mountains of all sorts of geological structures and ages. The central plain is mostly bogland, with glacial deposits of clay and of sand, and scarred by hundreds of lakes.

The Lake of Glencar, with its sparkling waterfalls above left and lush surrounding countryside left, was beloved of the Sligo poet, W. B. Yeats.

Above right is shown the Burren; right the curious outline of Benbulben Mountain, one of the most prominent summits of the Dartry Mountains, in Co. Sligo, and overleaf majestic Slieve League, the highest sea cliff in Europe, in Co. Donegal.

IRELAND

Scenically, Ireland is allied to Scotland and to Wales, but lost out, for good or evil, on coalfields.

With over eight hundred lakes and rivers, the land is well watered and beautified. The Shannon River is the longest, at 230 miles, and drains one-fifth of the whole of Ireland. A bird's-eye view of the topography shows the Shannon flowing from north to south, through Lough Allen, Lough Ree and Lough Derg. To the west are Loughs Mask and Corrib. North of the Shannon source lie the Lower and Upper Lough Erne. Lough Neagh dominates the north-eastern corner with its Bann and Lagan rivers. The Boyne and the Liffey flow east – west. The Slaney, Barrow, Nore and Suir flow to the south-east, the Blackwater and Lee flow from the west to turn to the south. Lough Leane peeps out from the deep south-western corner.

Carrantuohill is the highest mountain peak in the country at 3,414 feet, while Lough Neagh is the largest lake, at 153 square miles.

The south and south-westerly regions have areas of old red sandstone rocks with valleys of limestone. The west features limestone deserts, plus a mixture of granite, quartzite and igneous rocks. This is repeated in the north-east, where great basalt plateaux appear with the addition of granite mountains. Granite reappears in the east coast.

Twice Ireland was subjected to ice ages of glaciation, the first covering the entire country, the second extending to two-thirds of the country. The

IRELAND

retreat of the glaciers has given ice-smoothed rocks, and glacial deposits of clay and gravel, providing a distinct character to the landscape.

Because of Ireland's position in Europe as the last country to suffer the last ice age, much of the earlier fauna and flora disappeared, and consequently there is much less in Ireland than in Britain, but it is also somewhat different, as Cantabrian plants, such as are found in Spain, are also found in Ireland, and even some North American types. Snakes, moles and weasels are not found in Ireland, as they are in England, and fewer types of mice. The Irish hare is nothing like the English hare, but has more in common with the Scottish hare. It is unusually large.

One area in the west of Ireland has rare alpine Arctic species of wild flowers, and the south-west flora is rich in Mediterranean species. The bird life of Ireland is also rich, there being 380 species of wild birds, of which over 130 breed in the country. Three-quarters of the world's Greenland white-fronted geese spend their winters in Ireland, and the Atlantic coast gives safe harbour to most of the world's gannets and stormy petrels.

Co. Mayo encompasses some of the finest coastal scenery, from sandy beaches such as that off Achill Island above, to majestic, rugged headlands, evidenced in Crew Bay as a solitary boat is reflected in the glassy waters above far right, as well as miles of unspoilt countryside dotted with picturesque cottages right. Ballina above right, a noted trout and salmon angling centre on the River Moy, is the county's largest town, whilst Ashford Castle below far right, formerly the country seat of the Guinness family, has received the coveted Egon Ronay award as the best hotel in both Britain and Ireland.

From the geographical location, its climate, its geological structure, its flora and fauna, emerges what might best be described as the anatomy of the landscape, so characteristic of Ireland, so different from, for example, that of England, which makes for an Irish scenery unaffected by an Industrial Revolution, which in turn has shaped the environment which produced its effects on the people who came to inhabit this off-shore island. This least populated country in Europe has today a population of approximately 4,700,000. They are, in the main, what might best be described as white Europeans, of many racial mixtures, the majority of whom, for historical reasons, could be described as Nordic. Being Irish, they have, of course, to be paradoxically different; so many brown-haired people have blue eyes, and many fair-haired people have brown eyes, and about one in twenty is a red-head.

It is impossible to say precisely when the first people came to the island of Ireland, or from whence they originally came. But concerning the earliest inhabitants, occasionally one comes across a historical quotation which is particularly apt and timeless.

IRELAND

Concerning the early Celts, the Roman historian, Diodorus Siculus, who was a contemporary of Julius Caesar, made one very discerning statement. He wrote some forty books of history in Rome, of which some fourteen survive, and while he is not thoroughly reliable, he wrote of the Celts as follows: –

'Physically the Celts are terrifying in appearance, with deep-sounding and very harsh voices. In conversation they use few words and speak in riddles, for the greater part hinting at things and leaving a great deal to be understood. They frequently exaggerate in order to promote themselves at the expense of others. They are boasters and threateners, and given to boastful self-dramatisation, and yet they are quick of mind with good natural ability for learning.' Diodorus Siculus goes on to say that the Celts have bards or poets, who sometimes indulge in satire, and sometimes in praise. From this comparatively early, but Roman quotation, it would seem that the early Celts had much in common with their ancestors of today; the Irish people, who still speak in riddles.

When it comes to the history of the Celtic peoples, and the earliest inhabitants of Ireland, you pay your money to the history experts, and take your choice. Some say the early Irish language had its origins in Sanskrit, and that the earliest Celtic serpentine designs had their origins in India, or even Persia.

The early Celts controlled all Europe as far as the Danube, including Budapest, Paris, Belgrade and Lyons. The Roman Legions, with their iron discipline, broke the power of what were to them the 'barbaric' Celts, i.e. they did not speak Latin. The Imperial policy of divide and rule put an end to these war-like warriors, with the only exception that Roman civilisation never crossed the sea to Ireland. This was ultimately Ireland's gain, as she missed the Roman military occupation, with its straight Roman military roads, driven through the virgin forests like

Lough Conn, set in North Mayo between Foxford, Pontoon and Ballina, is pictured above right; right and above far right the Sheefry Hills as they preside dramatically over south-west Mayo and Delphi, and below centre right and below far right, heather-covered Achill, the largest island off the Irish coast, joined to the mainland only by a bridge.

modern motorways, linking military fort to military fort. Ireland did not enjoy the doubtful benefits of Roman 'Law and Order', which crucified all opposition with the mailed fist of a totalitarian state, more often than not headed by power-hungry or insane military generals. They missed Roman sanitation, hot baths, piped water, vomitoriums, mosaic floors and cool villas, and the law and order of the grave-yard. The naked Celtic warrior was his own man, an individualist; unity with his neighbours was never his strong point.

The Southern part of Ireland had, geographically, sea routes and links with the Celts of Gaul and Spain, the Bretons and the Basques, and there was constant coming and going in wares between the Celts of Wales and of Ireland, who could look across the Irish Sea at each other's mountain peaks. The nearest Celts were just across the sea in Scotland, a mere ten miles away.

Celtic Ireland was Gaelic speaking, and the many invasions of Ireland by Celtic peoples from Britain and from the Continent took place finally in four phases, between 600 BC and 100 BC. The first were the Picts, followed by

IRELAND

the Fir Bolg – who came from Continental Europe – followed by the invaders who founded Leinster and Connacht. The oldest Gaels, from Scotland, founded Ulster, and the fourth Gaelic division of Ireland was the Province of Munster.

Although the Romans regarded the Celts as barbarians, this Gaelic-speaking race of fighting men had a highly developed civilisation of its own, in addition to its own language. Its society was led by petty kings and princes or chieftains, who in turn were supported by the modern equivalent of law-makers, recorders of history, Druidic priests and magicians and, most important of all, a bardic class, or class of poets. Since the very beginning of the Celtic nation, poets who could break a man by ridicule, or make him by praise, were mighty powerful in the Gaelic society. Magic and poetry went hand in hand, and poets were also all-powerful as soothsayers, or seers, or wielders of supernatural and visionary powers. Kings and princes and petty chieftains needed genealogical support for their power, and for the boosting of their families, and the bards always obliged in filling up the

Sumptuously furnished, the hall above and library right reveal the impressiveness of Westport House, a fine example of Georgian architecture, which is the home of the Marquis of Sligo, and above right is shown the delightful interior of Clonalis House, the family home of the O'Connor Don.

Set in Ireland's glorious Lakeland is Lough Key Forest Park above left, whilst picturesque Derravarra Inn, Butlersbridge, Cavan left, is said to serve the best pub food in Ireland.

IRELAND

gaps, going as far back as Adam and Eve for ancestry, if necessary. The heritage was in the spoken word, and the written word came much later. History really begins with the written word, the first written words being largely concerned with heroic stories and legends, the exploits of warriors and the loves of kings and queens.

In these earliest days there were no real High Kings of All-Ireland, but there was a multiplicity of small kings, each with his own 'tuath' or 'tribe', a small realm based on a society of kinship. It was a male-dominated world; a pagan tribal system with a highly developed sense of law and justice, and it produced masterpieces of art from its ranks of craftsmen in metal and leather, and wood and stone.

The worship of the early Celts is obscure and mysterious. They certainly had gods of the sun and of the sea, and held an overwhelming superstition of the nature of the world around them, in rocks and rivers, stones and trees, mountains and clouds, and in the elements. Living on a western Atlantic seaboard, their whole life was bent by the winds and gales, storms and rain clouds, and sunbursts, in the forever changing movement of clouds and skies from west to

Rich in historic interest, exemplified in Muireadach's Cross above, a relic of the 5th-century university at Monasterboice, and the fascinating exhibits below far right in the Rothgory Transport Museum, Dunleer, the particular beauty of Co. Louth is revealed in the mountainous Cooley peninsula above right and overleaf. Right can be seen the Nuremore Hotel golf course, Co. Monaghan, and above far right two friends going to Belmullet market in Co. Mayo.

east. They were a sensuous people, fully in tune with mother earth.

Perhaps a bloodthirsty lot, they had no tremendous regard as warriors for their own skin, and flung themselves into battle without a qualm or fear of death. This bravado in battle, and almost throw-away attitude to death, as long as it was in a worthwhile encounter, appears to have been a basic attitude of the Celtic warrior. Basically 'one far fierce hour and sweet' was preferable to a lifetime of humdrum mediocrity. Lurking always in the Celtic mind was the concept that it was the man who endured the most who was the victor, not the man who inflicted the most, and the individual conscience concerning this ultimately became accepted by the majority as the philosophy of political endurance, and survival.

Interest in our Celtic heritage was seriously shown by Irish scholars in Victorian times, who were searching for 'roots'. More often than not, even with great scholarship behind them, they took the romantic view that the Celts were all '...a mighty race, taller than Roman spears', of bearded, heavily armed warriors, with trews or saffron kilts, holding gigantic Irish

IRELAND

wolf-hounds on leashes, the sun bursting from the heavens, the older warriors playing chess, listening to the sound of harps, or pipes, or the declaiming of poets, or bards, and stately Irish matrons and maidens in adoring attendance, with great sides of venison, wild boar, salmon, trout, or what-have-you, at the table, while the 'Uisce Beatha' – the 'water of life' – flowed gently, but not too freely, and the forerunners of modern tourists thronged the festive board for free.

Celtic life was not quite as simple as that, of course, but at least when the professional warriors went to war with each other there was no great loss of life, and ordinary life went on with minor 'Donnybrooks' in the background. The entire tribe was not involved while a few head of cattle were lost or won, or a wife or two, or a supposed wrong righted. As ever, this Celtic society was a hotbed of lawyers interpreting the 'Brehon Laws' with all the arts and skills of modern Senior Counsels or, as they are called in the North of Ireland, Queen's Counsellors. Forever arguing, for the sheer sake and pleasure of discussion, the Great Gaels in their democracy of elected kings and princes, did a great trade in slaves, and were utterly devoted to the tribal ownership of land. The whole history of Ireland is wrapped up with the question of land for the people, and the cynics will say that after centuries of fighting for the possession of their lands, the people did not over-exert themselves in the tilling of their soil. It was enough to have won it, and to hold it, and to guard it jealously against land-hungry neighbours, or foreigners.

However, to talk of 'Celts' with a Gaelic language, conscious of a land called 'Ireland' is to jump ahead some thousands of years.

The very first people to come to Ireland came between 6,000 and 5,000 BC, after the Ice Age, and were coastal fishermen and gatherers of food. Shells and stone axes mark some of their dwelling places, and while their homes are lost, their tombs remain and are many. From pre-Christian times one can trace up to 40,000 forts, raths or 'fairy rings' throughout the length and breadth of modern Ireland. Archaeologically, Ireland is the wealthiest country in Europe, because modern industrialisation and urbanisation have not blotted out the landscape or concreted over man's antiquities. The earliest

tombs were megalithic, that is made of 'great stones'. The most mysterious and mystic of the counties of Ireland is County Sligo, whose landscape abounds in these earliest types of burial chambers.

The Boyne Valley has the most spectacular Passage-Grave tombs in the country, at Newgrange, Dowth and Knowth. Literally, there is a passage into the heart of the mound, and within the stone-roofed mound, a central chamber with burial stones and basins, in many cases highly decorated with Oriental motifs. Bodies were cremated before burial in the tombs.

In addition to these Passage-Graves, there are hundreds of Druidic altars, known as Dolmens. These are enormous standing stones, superimposed on which are huge flat stones roofing the whole. These must surely mark the last resting place of great chiefs or leaders. In addition to these Passage-Graves and Dolmens, there are numerous 'Crannogs' or lake dwelling forts. As in many parts of Europe, there are plenty of stone circles and

Pictured above is a rowing boat half-concealed among the reeds of Lough Owel; above left the River Blackwater as it meanders through lush parkland and wooded valleys in the Royal County of Meath; left and below far left Headford House, the estate of the Marquis of Headford, which lies in wooded land a few miles outside the town of the same name, and above far left the interior of Tullynally Castle, formerly Pakenham Hall, near Castlepollard, the residence of Lord Longford.

IRELAND

pillar stones. These last-mentioned, tall standing stones, are frequently marked by 'Ogham' writing, the earliest form of writing in Ireland. Lines are cut in the stone across a basic line, and the Gaelic names of once famous chiefs and leaders are simply commemorated.

Ireland's Bronze Age, a thousand years before Christ, and as recent as 500 BC, produced some of the most beautiful copper, bronze and gold work in Europe. Hill forts and ring forts sheltered families and their cattle, and one of the most striking of these is the Grianan of Aileach in County Donegal. This is breathtaking in its setting, overlooking Loughs Foyle and Swilly. The walls are 13 feet thick and over 70 feet in diameter. It is an immense ramparted fort and to stand within this stone circle is to sense the

presence of the pagan gods of legendary times, and of a people of long ago.

It is only rivalled in its awesomeness by the Fort of Dun Aenghus, on the Aran Islands in County Galway. Set on a cliff edge, with a 200-foot drop into the raging waters of the Atlantic Ocean, this has three half circles of stone wall defences. Beyond these defences of the most westerly fortress in Europe is a field of thousands upon thousands of standing stones, like the earliest form of tank trap in the world. The earliest people picked their fortified dwellings in strategic places, often siting them on promontories of land where sea and cliffs and high lands would make for natural defences.

Possibly the most famous single stone in Ireland is the Turoe Stone in County Galway, highly decorated with Celtic curvilinear designs. This is clear

evidence of La Tène Celts dwelling in Ireland about one hundred years before Christ. The Turoe Stone is at Bullaun, near Loughrea. This stone originally stood beside the ring-fort of Feerwore.

A Celtic Ireland, with four historic provinces of Ulster, Munster, Leinster and Connacht (Ulster being predominant in actual power) and divided into about one hundred and fifty small kingships, was fully ready for Christianity, when it came from Rome, via Britain, first in the person of Palladius, a bishop sent by Pope Celestine, followed by Saint Patrick, who became the patron saint of Ireland by virtue of his extraordinary successful missionary work in converting the pagan kings and princes and populace to Christ. He himself had been captured by raiding pirates, and brought to Ulster as a slave. He escaped back to his native Britain, urged by a calling to convert the native Irish to Christ, and returned as a missionary bishop. To the credit of the Celts they made no martyrs among the missionaries, they very simply went head over heels into the Christian faith with all the fervour of the early Church, and of the desert fathers. They were hermit-like by nature and environment.

The Golden Age of Ireland then followed, when the country was bursting with monastic foundations, universities of great learning, where the faith was kept alive, and ultimately taken back by Irish missionaries to Britain, to Gaul, to Germany, until the whole of Europe was restored from its barbarism to civilisation. This was 6th, 7th and 8th century Ireland, and the monuments, proof, are still to be seen today in the ruins of monastic-university settlements, the round towers, the Celtic crosses and, later, the great art treasures, such as the Book of Kells and Saint Patrick's bell shrine, the Ardagh Chalice and the Cross of Cong.

The round towers, many still stand-

Familiar scenes in diverse Co. Galway, where the Connemara landscape is noted for its breathtaking beauty overleaf, include turf stacking, aided by the sturdy Connemara ponies above left, and sheep shearing right; harvesting in the rural Tuam region above right, and time-honoured net-repairing, an all-too-familiar task of fishermen, on a sandy beach in the Aran Islands left.

IRELAND

Sightseers are pictured above at *Dungloe, Co. Donegal; Ballynahinch, a charming Connemara lake in the heart of the famous Martin country below; traditional cottages amid the Connemara landscape above and below far right, and near Leenane, Co. Galway, above right; tidal fishing for salmon and sea trout at Renvyle below right; a craft shop in Connemara above centre right; the grounds of the Renvyle House Hotel, Co. Galway below centre right, and magnificent Kylemore Abbey by the shores of Pollacappal Lough in Co. Galway overleaf.*

ing today, are unique architecturally to Ireland. Approximately 100 feet in height, round and with a pointed conical top, they date from the ninth century, and were bell towers, look-out towers, and places of defence and refuge from the raiding Norsemen. The entrance doors, high above ground level, were reached by rope or ladder, and sacred vessels, books and valuables were stored safely during hit-and-run raids on the coast and the estuaries. There are seventy still standing, many of them on the sites of former university monastic settlements.

The famous Celtic crosses date from the tenth to the thirteenth century, and many are remarkable for their stone-carved, scriptural scenes. They were the visual aids of their day to Christian teaching.

A brief glance at the history of Ireland, after her glorious Golden Age, shows that the Vikings progressed from hit-and-run raids to the permanent settlement of towns such as Dublin, and engaged heavily in trade, including the slave trade. Came the Normans, in the eleventh and twelfth centuries, who, like their Norse relations and predecessors, became absorbed into the nation. The old Gaelic power, headed by the Ulster chiefs, was broken once and for all at the Battle of Kinsale in 1601, and the roots put down for future problems by the confiscation of lands from the people, and the 'planting' of loyal English and Scottish Protestant colonists, who remained a beleaguered garrison force aloof from the native Irish. From then on, the Irish Parliament was subject to the English Parliament.

From the eighteen hundreds until the nineteen twenties, insurrections, albeit unsuccessful, were the order of the day, alongside a nineteenth century use of the Irish representation in the British Parliament. No nation in Europe has a monopoly of suffering, or starvation, or oppression, but Ireland certainly endured her worst times in the 1840's famine, which decimated her population by starvation, and drove millions to seek a new life in Britain, and notably in the United

States of America.

When the democratic process failed to procure Home Rule through Westminster, the young men took to arms, and in 1916, after the rising of the poets, and the citizen army, public opinion swung behind the young Republicans. After a vicious guerrilla war between the forces of the Crown and the Irish Republican forces, a Treaty was signed, under duress, and modern Ireland finished up with an 'Irish Free State' of twenty-six counties and a 'Northern Ireland' made up of six of the historic nine counties of the Province of Ulster. This latter had its own Parliament for fifty years. Came civil rights agitation from the under-represented section of the people, a dubiously treated minority, and fresh political problems, as yet unresolved, arose. At present, Northern Ireland is under the direct rule of Westminster, and is part of the United Kingdom.

Eventually, men of goodwill, of patience, tolerance, mutual respect and understanding, will write another chapter, and a happy one, in the history of an ever youthful, vibrant nation, which plays its part in the heart of the European Community, and in the United Nations.

The Counties of Ireland

Ireland today retains its four ancient provinces of Leinster, Munster, Connacht and Ulster. Politically, twenty-six counties comprise the Republic, and of the nine counties of Ulster, six – Antrim, Down, Armagh, Derry, Tyrone and Fermanagh make up Northern Ireland. Ulster, in the north, is made up of nine counties, Leinster in the east, twelve counties, Connacht, in the west, five counties, and Munster in the south, six counties.

Any journey through Ireland is best done as long ago by the High Kings. They swept around the countryside clockwise, commencing in the east, down to the south and south-west, up the west coast, and then around the north. In theory as in history, the greatest power lay for a long time in Ulster, with Leinster a seat of central

IRELAND

authority, which did not cover the whole country, and with Munster and Connacht the remotest from central control.

Dublin County is much unexplored by the modern-day traveller, and still contains many pleasant surprises. North of Dublin lies the land of the Fair Strangers, the Norsemen, whose descendants include the hospitable and hard-working market gardeners and fishermen of Rush, and Skerries. Saint Patrick is associated with the island named after him, near Skerries, and Baldongan Castle, three miles distant, is a former power centre of the myster-ious and secret society of the Norman Knights Templar. At Lusk is a sixth century round tower, in a state of perfect preservation, to which has been added a square Norman tower. At Swords is another round tower, where once stood the monastery of Saint Colmcille. From the top of the hill of Howth there is a spectacular pano-ramic view of Dublin Bay, with the Wicklow mountains to the south and the mountains of Mourne to the north. In this area, too, is one of the earliest churches in the country, the Church of Saint Doulagh, near Portmarnock.

South of Dublin is the town of Dun Laoghaire, 'The Fort of Leary', the main harbour for Dublin. There is an appropriate monument to George IV at the harbour, to commemorate his visit in 1821 when the town was, on this occasion, given the royal title of 'Kings-town'. The Martello Tower at Sandy-cove, now a museum, was the one-time home of James Joyce and his cronies. Killiney Bay is said to be the Naples of Ireland because of its hill and pano-ramic background of mountains, and its fine sweep of bay.

Adjacent to Dublin County is the Garden of Ireland, County Wicklow, with rolling green countryside,

wooded glens and valleys, and low-lying mountains. At Powerscourt are the world-famous gardens, and at Glendalough is the famous monastic settlement of Saint Kevin, dating from the sixth century. The magnificent round tower still stands from the ninth century, guarding the blue lakes – Glendalough means 'the Glen of the Two Lakes'. The poet-musician-singer, Thomas Moore, made the Vale of Avoca and its village famous in his melody the 'Meeting of the Waters'.

West Wicklow has the charming vil-lage of Blessington, and nearby the huge lake of Pollaphuca, which sup-plies Dublin city with water and elec-trical energy.

County Wexford, sweeping round the south-eastern corner of Ireland, is

The Cross of the Scriptures above; O'Rourke's Tower left and the Nun's Church above right are sited at Clonmacnoise, one of Ireland's most celebrated holy places. Shown right is the magnificent residence of the Earl and Countess of Rosse, and overleaf Hough's Pub, in Banagher.

340

the meeting place of the Irish Sea and the Atlantic Ocean. It is a county of great agricultural tradition, long sandy beaches and broad rivers. The beach at Courtown consists of over two miles of sand, and a few miles away are the sandy beaches of Ballymoney and the delightful coves of Pollshone and of Ardamine. At Ferns, Saint Aidan founded his monastery in the sixth century; later, for a short time, this became the capital of the Kings of Leinster.

Five miles or so from the historic town of Ferns is the village of Boolavogue, which was the scene of a famous insurrection sparked off by the burning of a local chapel. The ballad named after the village has become one of the historic and poignant songs of Ireland, and was loved and much sung and favoured by John F. Kennedy, a former President of the United States. Enniscorthy, in the valley of the River Slaney, is now more famous for its Strawberry Fair than its stormy history. Enniscorthy Castle, dated 1586, was built by the Norman adventurer, Raymond le Gros, then became

IRELAND

the property of the MacMurrough Kavanaghs, who gave it to the Franciscans, who were forced to part with it to the Elizabethan poet, Edmund Spencer. At Vinegar Hill, east of the town, the insurrection sparked off in Boolavogue, in 1798, came to a disastrous and cruel end when the untrained peasant army, with its long barrelled duck guns and home-made pikes, fell to professional red-coats and Hessian mercenaries.

Wexford, the capital of the county, is a picturesque town on the mouth of the Slaney, part fishing village, part almost mediaeval, and the home of some of the most talented and kindly people in Ireland. While battles long ago may be remembered in more than a few famous ballads, the town today has world fame as the centre for an international Festival of Opera. A statue of Commodore Barry, founder of the United States Navy, looks out over the harbour. At Dunganstown, not far from New Ross, is the original cottage home of the great-grandfather of John F. Kennedy.

Across the bridge from Wexford

Castletown above and above left, one of Ireland's greatest Palladian Mansions, is headquarters of the Irish Georgian Society. Founded in the 12th century, majestic St Patrick's Cathedral, Dublin, is shown right, and left adjoining Marsh's Library, the country's oldest public library.

IRELAND

Town is Ferrycarrig, the site of an ancient castle where the first Norman invader, Robert Fitzstephen, set up his centre of power with his freebooters. The world can be grateful to Wexford for its wildfowl reserve, where half the Greenland white-fronted geese of the world spend their winter months. Off the coast are the Saltee Islands, one of the largest bird sanctuaries in the country.

Kilkenny, from the Irish for 'Canice's Church', a sixth century monastic foundation, still maintains today a liberal and progressive Christian outlook, and is the headquarters of the Design Centre of Ireland. It is a handsome city, with its thirteenth century cathedral, its magnificent castle of the Butlers, the Dukes of Ormonde, and a college which produced Dean Swift, Congreve, Berkeley and Farquhar. In its heyday it was the city of an independent sixteenth century Irish parliament, complete with Papal Nuncio. The cathedral boasts a round tower. Kilkenny is a rich, much under-rated county, whose valleys of the River Nore and of the River Barrow are vales of quiet beauty. The hills of Slieveardagh and of Booley make for attractive uplands. One of the jewels of the county is Jerpoint Abbey, founded in 1158 by the King of Ossory, Donagh MacGillapatrick. It is the finest monastic ruin in the country.

Adjacent to the county of Kilkenny is the county of Carlow, to the north-east. Barely 300 miles square it is nearly the smallest county in Ireland, which, of course, is 'the wee county', County Louth. With the help of the River Slaney, and of the River Barrow, it has a rich fertile limestone land, and the landscape has soft-shaped hills and a great greenness.

The county capital is Norman, and the countryside has memorials four thousand years old, such as the Dolmen at Browne's Hill, two miles from Carlow, with the largest capstone in Europe, twenty feet square, five feet thick and weighing one hundred tons.

Inland counties of Ireland are all too often neglected, or overlooked, by people speeding through them to somewhere else, and County Kildare is one such county. West of Dublin, it has been the horse land of sporting, racing and hunting people since before the time of Christ. The rolling grasslands, over limestone plains, produce the greatest race horses in the world.

The national stud is there, and the finest Georgian mansion in the country, Castletown House, now the headquarters of the Georgian Society of Ireland. The Curragh is the leading race track, and on this course each year is held the Irish Derby, which carries one of the largest prize monies of any classic in Europe.

Three places spring to mind at the mention of Kildare: Celbridge, once the home of Esther Vanhomrigh, Jonathan Swift's tragic Vanessa; Maynooth, with its college of Saint Patrick, one of the largest and most conservative Catholic seminaries in the world, and Conolly's Folly, near Celbridge, one of the most obscene wastes of money and labour by a worthless and useless landlord class.

The county of Laois, flat, save for the Slieve Bloom mountains, has as its main town Port Laois – 'the fort of Laoghis' – and was originally called Maryborough after its settlement by Bloody Mary in her attempt to subdue the clan of the O'Mores.

Offaly, the adjacent county, in addition to its fame for 'Tullamore Dew', the Irish equivalent of Dram-

Dublin by night, as the city lights cast glimmering reflections along the River Liffey left, is contrasted with the bustling, day-time activity on O'Connell Street, the main thoroughfare, as it crosses the river by O'Connell Bridge right, whilst beneath a misty dawn sky stand The Four Courts above right. The Custom House above, topped by a superb dome, is considered to be Dublin's finest public building.

IRELAND

buie, has, on the banks of the Shannon, one of the most famous holy places in Ireland, Clonmacnois, the monastery and university city founded by Saint Ciaran in the year 548 AD. The stone Cross of the Scriptures is one of the most ornate of all Celtic crosses, and the whole area is a riot of stone crosses, early grave slabs and sites of ancient churches and cathedrals.

The county of Westmeath, with its many wooded lakes and rivers, is famous for its 'Goldsmith Country' near Lough Ree, described in his 'The Deserted Village'; and for the town of Athlone, where John Count McCormack, one of the world's greatest tenors, was born.

Longford, a small county of lakes, rivers and farms, is forever associated with Edgeworthstown; the famous family whose members included

Maria Edgeworth, first settled there, and their family vault is in the attractive and well-kept Church of Saint John. Goldsmith, too, is associated with this county, which gave him the idea for his play 'She Stoops to Conquer'.

The county of Meath, 'Royal' Meath, was the seat of pagan and Christian kings at historic Tara, and it was on the Hill of Slane that Saint Patrick lit the Paschal Fire. Trim, Navan and Kells

are the best-known historic towns, and Kells was the monastic settlement of Saint Colmcille of the sixth century.

The round tower at Kells is 100 feet high, and the most valuable book in the world, the Book of Kells, was produced in this monastic settlement. The Celtic crosses in the area are exceedingly ornate.

County Lough, the smallest county in the country, just over 300 square miles, has the distinction of being associated with one of the great epics of ancient Ireland, the Táin Bó Cuailgne – 'The Cattle Raid of Cooley'. It is rich in historic monuments and noted for its Cistercian Abbey ruins of Mellifont, founded by Saint Malachi, the Irish friend of the great Saint Bernard of Clairvaux. It is equally famous for the fifth century monastery of Monasterboice – 'Saint Buithe's Abbey' – where Muireadach's cross is one of the most exquisite stone carvings of the earliest Christian period.

Pictured above, below left *and* above far left *is the* Dublin Spring Show; above left *the famous* Irish Derby *at the* Curragh of Kildare, below far left *hurling at* Croke Park, *and overleaf a trawler as it sets out from* Howth, *a popular beauty spot in Co. Dublin.*

IRELAND

South-west of the Province of Leinster are the six counties of the Province of Munster, beginning with Waterford, adjacent to Wexford and Kilkenny. A county of rivers, the Suir and the Blackwater, its prides are the Comeragh mountains and a rugged coastline. The city of Waterford is a Norse-Norman foundation and it has given many distinguished leaders of thought and of action to the nation. Ard-

County Cork, the largest county in Ireland, has probably produced more brains, beauty and talent per square acre than any other county in Ireland. With an enormous indented Atlantic coastline, and with one of the most spectacular waterways, the Blackwater, its capital city was founded by Saint Finbarr as a monastic university in the sixth century, and near this original site the present-day University

College, Cork, stands. A 'Rebel' city, Cork has always given the lead to the nation. Five miles from the city is the village and castle of Blarney, with its famous stone, said to give the gift of eloquence to all who kiss it. To the east of Cork is the village of Youghal, famous for the house in which Sir Walter Raleigh lived, and which still stands today. Kinsale, to the south, once one of the most important British naval ports,

more, on the sea, was the seventh century monastery of Saint Declan, and is marked by a perfectly preserved round tower. Lismore Castle, on the River Blackwater, is one of the most attractive-looking in Ireland, and dates back over the centuries to an early Christian monastery, taken over by King John, and then by the rapacious Sir Walter Raleigh and the Earl of Cork 'Boyles Law' family.

Covering 14,000 acres, the celebrated gardens of Powerscourt, in Co. Wicklow right and overleaf, are adorned with ornamental lakes, bridges, tessellated pavements and statuary which provided an idyllic setting for its 18th-century mansion.

is associated with William Penn, founder of the State of Pennsylvania and one time Clerk of the Admiralty Court of Kinsale.

West Cork revels in wild and rugged scenery and becomes an area of warm beauty and soft Mediterannean-type flora and fauna in places such as Bantry Bay, Glengarriff, Gougane Barra and the Beara Peninsula.

The county next door, Kerry, is a blend of mountains and cliffs and spectacular Atlantic headlands. Always the most remote south-westerly county in Ireland, it has kept to a high degree the ancient tradition of the country for hospitality, for learning and for strength of character. The Iveragh and Dingle Peninsulas are the next promontories to America, and the beauty of the lakes of Killarney has never ceased to capture the admiration of the world. It is very probable that Saint Brendan, known as 'The Navigator', set forth from Dingle and discovered the coast of America long before Columbus.

County Limerick, north of Kerry and Cork, and on the historic River Shannon, is so rich a county that it is known as 'The Golden Vale'. Originally a Danish settlement, the city of Limerick is a well preserved Irish town. In the country, twelve miles to the south of

the City, is Lough Gur, one of the most ancient dwelling places in the land. All the ages are recorded in the many stone monuments and remains of dwelling places, from Neolithic to Norman times. Across the broad estuary of the Shannon is the mighty limestone area of the Burren and the land of the 700-foot high Cliffs of Moher, and the fascinating strand of Lahinch, County Clare. This is O'Brien country, and the

Begun in 1740, Dublin's famous Phoenix Park above and above left, today includes about 1,760 acres of beautifully laid out gardens and trees. County Wicklow's tranquil parkland of the Vale of Clara left is set on the banks of the Avonmore River.

IRELAND

one-time haunt of the MacNamara Clan. The Burren landscape is like a moon-scape, but with an extraordinary range of flora, much of it Mediterranean and alpine.

There remains one more county to add to the list of Munster counties – one made famous by a World War I marching song – '*It's a long way to Tipperary*'. The mountain ranges of the Galtees and the Knockmealdowns are of great beauty, over 2,000 feet in

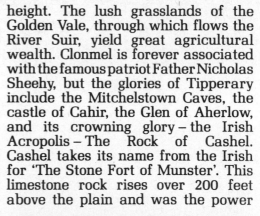

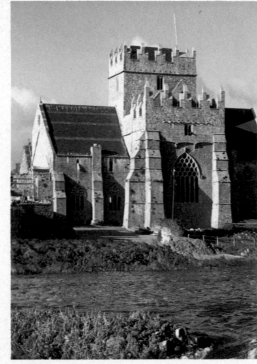

height. The lush grasslands of the Golden Vale, through which flows the River Suir, yield great agricultural wealth. Clonmel is forever associated with the famous patriot Father Nicholas Sheehy, but the glories of Tipperary include the Mitchelstown Caves, the castle of Cahir, the Glen of Aherlow, and its crowning glory – the Irish Acropolis – The Rock of Cashel. Cashel takes its name from the Irish for 'The Stone Fort of Munster'. This limestone rock rises over 200 feet above the plain and was the power

Once the seat of Munster kings, The Rock of Cashel can be seen above far left; left the Cistercian Hore Abbey, sited about half a mile west of the rock; above left The Abbey of the Holy Cross dating from the 11th century; top a reconstruction of a Bronze Age 'crannog' at Craggaunowen Castle, Co. Clare; above a forge in Bunratty Folk Park, and right Glenmacnass Valley with its tumbling river, in Co. Wicklow.

IRELAND

centre of the kings of Munster from the third until the eleventh century. Saint Patrick's Cross, Cormac's Chapel and towers show Irish church architecture at its peak.

'Walk Tall' might well be the motto of the men of Tipperary; mountain men who have contributed more than their share to the building of the nation. Slievenamon – 'The Mountain of the Women of Feimhinn' – is associated with the ancient legend of Diarmuid and Grainne, while at Holy Cross

stands the well-preserved and restored eleventh century Abbey.

Roscommon is one of Connacht's most lake-strewn counties. Entirely inland, it is bounded on its eastern side by the River Shannon and its lakes. Lough Key, with its forest park, is typical of the area. Lough Gara is rich in archaeological finds, ancient dugouts, crannogs, and a magnificent dolmen.

The hill of Rathcroghan is reputed to have been the power centre of Queen Maeve of Connacht, who features in the Ulster war saga of the 'Táin Bó Cuailgne' – 'The Cattle Raid of Cooley'. Probably a royal capital in its ancient days, it has nearby the Burial Place of the Kings, where Conn of a Hundred Battles and three famous queens, Banba, Fodhla and Eire lie. Dathi, an early Irish pagan king has his monument too.

Elphin was the birthplace of Oliver Goldsmith and Castlerea the birthplace of Sir William Wilde, father of Oscar Wilde. At Clonalis is a Victorian-looking mansion, Clonalis House, home of the O'Conor Don, a direct descendant of the last king of Ireland around 1169. The house is a treasure trove of historical documents, paintings, books and furnishings.

Leitrim is a lake-land county, and, because it is a relatively small county, on the borders of Sligo and Roscommon, is not as well known as its beauty deserves it to be. Lough Allen divides the county neatly in two parts.

IRELAND

Dromahair – 'The Ridge of the Two Air-Demons' – is the turbulent country of the Clan O'Rourke and recalls the intensely dramatic story of Dervorgilla, wife of Tiernan O'Rourke, who went off with Dermot MacMurrough, King of Leinster. This incident was the reason why the Anglo-Normans and their Welsh free-booters were invited from South Wales to 'assist' Dermot against his neighbouring chiefs, and so set in motion the Norman invasion of Ireland.

Little known, but of great beauty, are the Glencar waterfall and Lough, and the mountains of Truskmore and Cloghcorragh, and Lough Allen, seven miles long and three miles wide.

The county of Sligo, Yeats' country, has, on Lough Gill, near the town of Sligo, the lake-island of Innishfree, and a host of places associated with the poet. Lough Arrow is of equal beauty, and the whole area is steeped in great

In County Clare, where the broad Shannon estuary greets the great Atlantic Ocean, the diverse countryside offers unparalleled opportunities for a wide variety of recreational activities: above and opposite page above right Burke's Riding School, Newmarket-on-Fergus; trout fishing centre left and boating bottom left on Lough Inchiquin; opposite page above and below far left Bunratty Folk Park; opposite page below left a mediaeval banquet in Bunratty Castle, and top left sailing on the River Shannon at Killaloe.

IRELAND

antiquities, since from earliest times it was the coastal route for armies marching north and south.

Lough Gill has its megalithic tomb, and on top of Knocknarea is the tomb of Queen Maeve of Connacht. Over six hundred feet in circumference, and eighty feet high, it can be seen for miles around.

Drumcliff was the site of a monastery founded by Saint Columba in AD 574, and there is a magnificent early Celtic cross, and the grave of W. B. Yeats. The mountain of Benbulben dominates the county, and on its slopes died Diarmuid, the hero of the Diarmuid and Grainne love epic. Drumcliff was the scene of a famous early Christian battle which established the law of copyright. Three thousand men died fighting for Saint Columba versus Saint Finian in the 'Battle of the Books'. Finian had given Columba a loan of a psalter, and Columba made a copy from it, which Finian claimed as his

property. The matter was referred to the High King who, Solomon-wise, judged: 'To every cow its calf and to every book its copy'. The plain of Moytura was the scene of many, many battles in the centuries before Christ.

Galway county, lying on the Western Atlantic seaboard, is the chocolate-box colour photograph idea of everybody's Ireland, with its Twelve Bens of Connemara and its famous Lough Corrib. It is probable that Ptolemy referred to Galway city as 'Magnata'.

In Norman times the city became 'The City of the Tribes' – fourteen of them, and for many years the city traded with Spain, so that its buildings and people have a distinctive Spanish look. Off the coast are the Aran Islands, made famous in drama by J. M. Synge's 'Riders to the Sea', and in film in Flaherty's documentary 'Man of Aran'. Lough Corrib, seven miles wide and twenty-seven in length, dominates much of the country's scenery. At Clifden, on the edge of the sea, the first

east-west trans-Atlantic flight landed in 1919. Clonfert is a monastic settlement founded by Saint Brendan the Navigator in the fifth century. Not far from the town of Loughrea is the Turoe Stone, a perfect example of La Tene art of one hundred years before Christ. Coole Park is forever associated with Lady Gregory of the Abbey Theatre fame, Thoor Ballylee with W. B. Yeats, and Ballynahinch with 'Humanity Dick', the founder of the R.S.P.C.A.

IRELAND

The county of Mayo has a fantastic Atlantic coastline, a huge and magnificent off-shore island – Achill – and a lofty mountain – Croagh Patrick – Saint Patrick's Mountain, over 2,500 feet high. Clare Island was the fortress home of the Irish Pirate cum Sea Queen of the West – Grace O'Malley. At Westport is one of the finest stately homes in Ireland open to the public. Ballintubber Abbey has a history of uninterrupted service from the twelfth century until the present day. South

Adare Manor, Limerick previous page and above left, a 19th-century neo-Gothic style building, is the magnificent residence of the Earl of Dunraven. The historic village of Adare is also noted for its fine monastic ruins facing page which stand not far from the River Maigue. Beautifully illustrating Co. Kilkenny's rich, historic heritage is Kilkenny Castle above, built in the 13th century by the Norman gangster Strongbow, and Jerpoint Abbey left, founded in 1158 by the King of Ossory.

IRELAND

Moytura, plain of a thousand pre-Christian battles, merges with North Moytura in Sligo.

Of the nine counties of Ulster, Donegal, the most north-easterly, separated from its hinterland of Derry by the political borderline of Northern Ireland, is the jewel. It abounds in sweeping sandy beaches, washed by the Atlantic Ocean, and Donegal town was the seat of the O'Donnell Clan, of whom the most famous was Red Hugh. Lough Derg – the Red Lake – is the legendary penitential place of Saint Patrick. Lough Finn is the scene of ancient warrior sagas, and the Grianan of Aileach is an awesome circular stone fort, built nearly two thousand years before the birth of Christ. Saint Columcille was born on

the shores of Gartan Lough in AD 521. Mount Errigal, almost two and a half thousand feet high, and cone-shaped in gleaming white, looks for all the world like a volcanic mountain in Japan. For sheer beauty of mountain, lake, valley and peninsular coastline, Donegal is probably the most glamorous county in Ireland.

The county of Derry is part of the historic province of Ulster, and politically, today, part of the six counties of Northern Ireland. The capital city, Derry, or Londonderry as it became called when James I granted it to the Irish Society of London, was originally called Derry-Calgach, that is 'Calgach's Oak Wood'. Saint Columcille, perhaps better known throughout Europe as Saint Columbanus, set up a monastic foundation and university in AD 546, and cleared the original oak wood for his settlement. James I re-built the original city, and made it a walled city, which has survived the many vicissitudes of history. One of the most

famous of Irish traditional pieces of music is the 'Londonderry' or 'Derry' Air, which was first written down in Limavady, in the County of Derry, in 1851, from an itinerant fiddler.

It is a county of hills and lowlands in the north, and glens and valleys, with the Sperrin Mountains in the south. At Coleraine is the newest of Ireland's universities. The Northern Atlantic beaches are beautiful, and the county shares its borders with Donegal in the north-east, with Antrim in the east, and with Tyrone in the south. Coleraine is associated with Saint Patrick, and Maghera has its sixth century church of Saint Lurach.

Bordering Derry is the magnificent coastal county of Antrim, just thirteen miles from Torr Head across to the coast of Scotland. Lough Neagh, the largest lake in Ireland, or in Great Britain, takes up the west of the county, and the rest is fertile valleys and hills, and rising land. Belfast city, the capital of Northern Ireland, is an enormous

IRELAND

industrial area and port. The Antrim coastal road is one of the most attractive in the whole of Ireland, and the county retains its world fame for two things, the Irish whiskey distilled at Bushmills, and the extraordinary rock formation of cooled lava which constitutes the Giant's Causeway. It was on the mountain of Slemish that the slave boy, later to become Saint Patrick, spent six or so years tending sheep.

County Armagh, south of Antrim and Lough Neagh, is justly famous as 'The Garden of Ulster'. The town of Armagh – 'Ard Macha' – Macha's

Pictured above is tranquil Barley Cove, West Cork; top picturesque Dunmore East, Co. Waterford; above left the long, narrow peninsula of Hook Head, Co. Wexford; below left pretty Glandore, a Co. Cork resort; above centre left 13th-century Johnstown Castle, three miles south of Wexford; above far left Lady's Island, near Carnsore Point, once the site of a monastery dedicated to the Blessed Virgin; below far left beautiful Dunbrody Abbey, Co. Wexford, and overleaf magnificent Coumeenoole Strand on the Dingle Peninsula, in Co. Kerry.

IRELAND

Height, is named after the battling Queen Macha who, three hundred years before Christ, ruled from her royal palace at Eamhain Macha. Saint Patrick naturally chose this ancient town as his primatial see, and founded the monastic university of Armagh. Slieve Gullion, in South Armagh, nearly two thousand feet in height, is the site of Bronze Age burial places. Portadown is the breeding ground of some of the world's finest roses, and famous for its splendid apple crops.

County Monaghan shares the distinction with Counties Donegal and Cavan, of being south of the 'Border', and is a charming hilly lake-land, with well tended farms. This is the county of the Clan MacMahon, and the birthplace of the famous poet, Patrick Kavanagh. Near the town of Monaghan is Tydavnet, associated with Saint Dympna, daughter of a pagan king who ruled in this area which was historically part of the old kingdom of Oriel. In the west of the county is the town of Clones, one time a monastic settlement founded by Saint Tighearnach in the fifth century. The village of Inishkeen was the site of a monastery founded by Saint Deagh in the sixth century.

County Down is famous in ballad and song for its 'Star of the County Down', and its 'Mountains of Mourne'. It is a rich country, probably the most fertile land in the whole of Ireland, contrasted by the granite mountains of the Mourne. Eastwards, the peninsula of Ards forms a natural barrier between the sea and Strangford Lough. The coastal resorts of Bangor, Donaghadee, Newcastle and Warrenpoint line the eastern magnificent sea boundary of the county.

Holywood, six or so miles from Belfast, was originally the site of a church founded by the seventh century Saint Laserian. The Normans named it 'Sanctus Boscus' – the 'Holy Wood'.

County Kerry displays its varied, scenic beauty in Derrynane Bay, seen from Coomakista Pass above right; in breathtaking Cummeenduff or 'Black Valley' right; in renowned Killarney above far right, and in the ancient stones of the 12th-century Aghadoe Church below far right, whilst the 'Ring of Kerry' road provides spectacular views of the mountains overleaf as it encircles the Iveragh Peninsula.

Bangor – the 'Peaked Hill' – was originally a monastic foundation in the fifth century, of Saint Comgall. A major university city, its most illustrious graduate was Saint Columbanus, who founded monasteries throughout Europe, and another was Saint Gall, who brought Christianity to the Swiss. Some idea of the enormous size of this university settlement may be seen from the fact that when the Norsemen destroyed it in the eighth century, they put to the sword some three thousand people.

The Ards Peninsula is of great beauty, and Newtownards, a town of mediaeval origin, has on its eastern boundary the site of a monastery founded by Saint Finian, in the sixth century. The star of the county is, of course, Downpatrick – 'Dun Phadraig' – Saint Patrick's Fort. He founded his earliest church here. The saint landed at Saul, two miles north-east of Downpatrick in AD 432. It is said that Patrick died at Downpatrick; and the supposed site of his grave is marked by an enormous modern boulder of granite, into which has been cut the name 'Patric' and a cross.

Slieve Donard, nearly three thousand feet in height, is the highest of the Mountains of Mourne, and from its summit there is a view to the Isle of Man, to Scotland, to Donegal and to Wicklow.

County Tyrone is bounded on the north-east and north by counties Donegal and Derry, on the east by counties Antrim and Armagh, and in

IRELAND

the south-west by the counties of Fermanagh and Monaghan. This is O'Neill country, with every type of scenery, ranging from the 2,000 foot high Sperrin Mountains, to hills, river valleys and glens.

The O'Neills ruled from Dungannon – 'Gannon's Fort'. In the Clogher Valley lies the village of Clogher, which was the site of the Cathedral of Saint Macartan, a disciple of Saint Patrick. Near Cookstown is Killymoon Castle, a mansion designed by Nash, and a few miles away, south of Cookstown, is the territory of the O'Hagan Clan. To the east lies Ardboe, where Saint Colman of Dromore founded a monastery in the sixth century. It has one of the most outstanding Celtic crosses in Ulster.

The town of Omagh is set on the rivers Drumragh and Camowen, which join together to form the River Strule. The town of Strabane – 'The Fair River-Meadow', on the River Mourne, has many distinguished sons, not the least of whom was John Dunlap, who printed the American Declaration of Independence. The printing house of Gray's, where he learnt his printing trade, is still in existence.

County Cavan, part of the twenty-six counties of the Irish Republic, is the home of the O'Reilly Clan. It is lakeland countryside, with the River Erne rising in Lough Gowan on its way

Dating from 1784, quaint Ballycopeland Windmill above stands near the Island of the Mill. Above right can be seen the floodlit Belfast City Hall, designed by Bramwell Thomas and completed in Portland stone in 1906; right Stormont's Parliament Building; above far right Kilkeel Harbour, a quiet seaside resort in Co. Down, and below far right Bangor, one of Northern Ireland's principal yachting and boating centres.

North. Near the pretty town of Virginia, which is on the side of Lough Ramor, is Cuilcagh Lough, and in the house that once stood nearby, Cuilcagh House, Dean Swift sat down to begin his writing of 'Gulliver's Travels'. Cavan has produced many famous journalists, and at least two great generals, Field Marshal Thomas Brady of the Austrian Army, who became Governor of Dalmatia, born at Cootehill, and General Phil Sheridan, born at Killinkere, a commander-in-chief of the Army of the United States of America. On the west side of Cuilcagh Mountain is the 'Shannon Pot', the source of the mighty River Shannon.

What makes the county of Fermanagh so superbly different is that the River Erne covers a vast area with its Upper and Lower Loughs. Enniskillen, the home of the Maguire Clan, stands loftily in between the two beautiful lakes. It shares the Cuilcagh Mountain with its Cavan border, and north-west shares Lough Melvin. On the western border are the Upper and Lower Lough Macnean.

A few miles north of Enniskillen is Devenish Island on the Lower Lough Erne. Here is another Clonmacnoise,

with the sixth century monastery founded by Saint Molaise. There is a splendid round tower, eighty-five feet high, extensive monastic and mediaeval ruins, and a high cross. On White Island, north of Devenish, is an early church and sculptures. East of Enniskillen is Killadeas Church with seventh century carvings.

Belleek, on the Donegal border, is world-famous for its chinaware. West Fermanagh has limestone hills, and they contain some of the most complex cave systems in Ireland. Some nine miles south-west of Enniskillen is Florence Court, the beautiful demesne of the Earl of Enniskillen. With the County of Fermanagh the clock-wise circuit of the thirty-two counties of Ireland comes to an end.

Among County Antrim's many attractions are the White Rocks, vivid with sea pinks left; the wishing arch above right, one of the most spectacular of the coastal rock formations top; Carrickfergus Castle above, named after Fergus, the first king of Scotland who was drowned in the vicinity, and Ballintoy's famous Carrick-a-rede, or passage of the salmon right, a deep, 60-feet wide chasm through which the sea rushes clamorously.

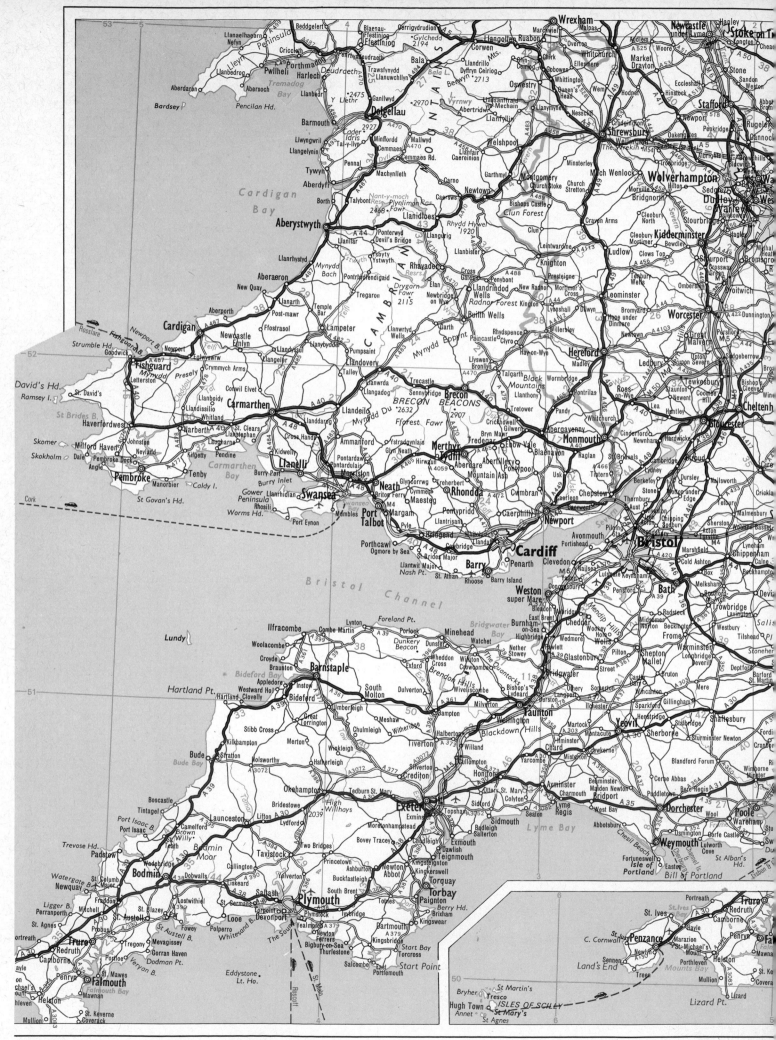

Distances in miles
between circled points   2   1:1 250 000   Heights in feet

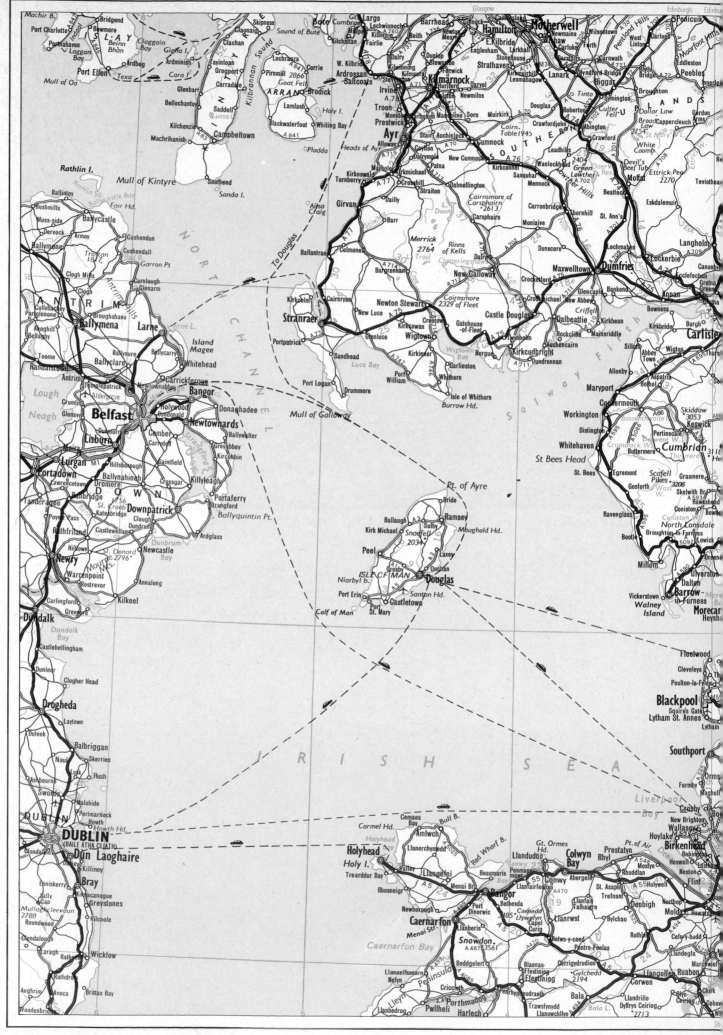

Distances in miles
between circled points   ⊙——11——⊙   1:1 250 000   Heights in feet

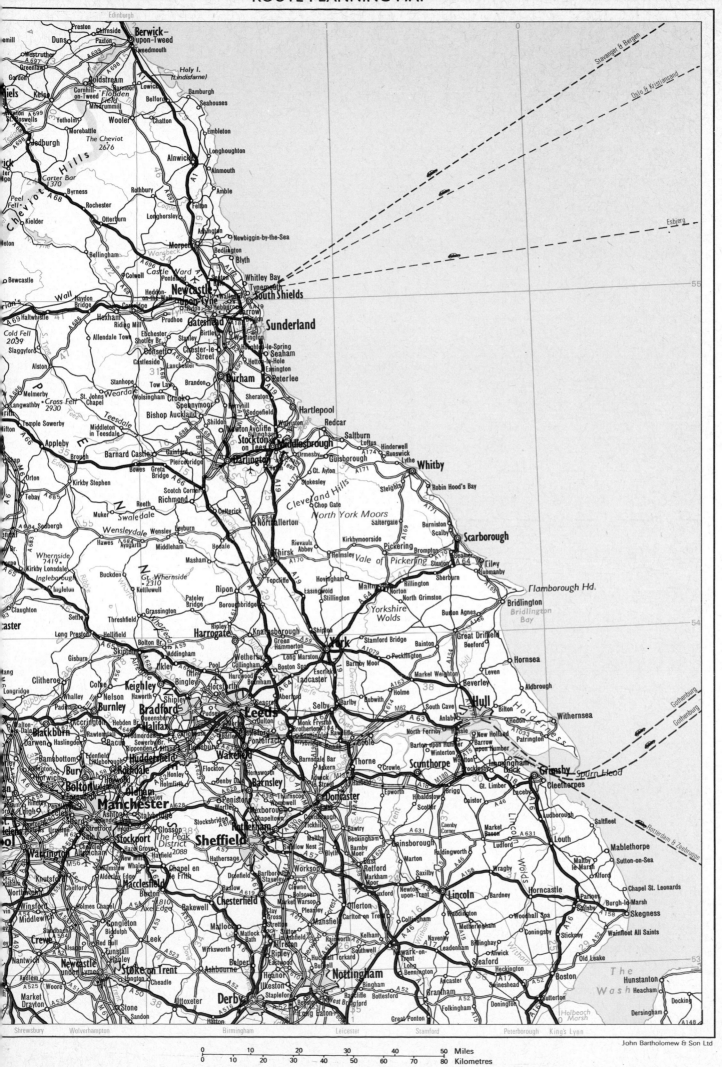

John Bartholomew & Son Ltd

| 0 | 10 | 20 | 30 | 40 | 50 | Miles |
| 0 | 10 20 | 30 40 | 50 60 | 70 80 | | Kilometres |

Heights in feet

1:1 250 000

Distance in miles
between circled points

ORKNEY

SHETLAND

N O R T H

S E A

0   10   20   30   40   50 Miles
0   10   20   30   40   50   60   70   80 Kilometres

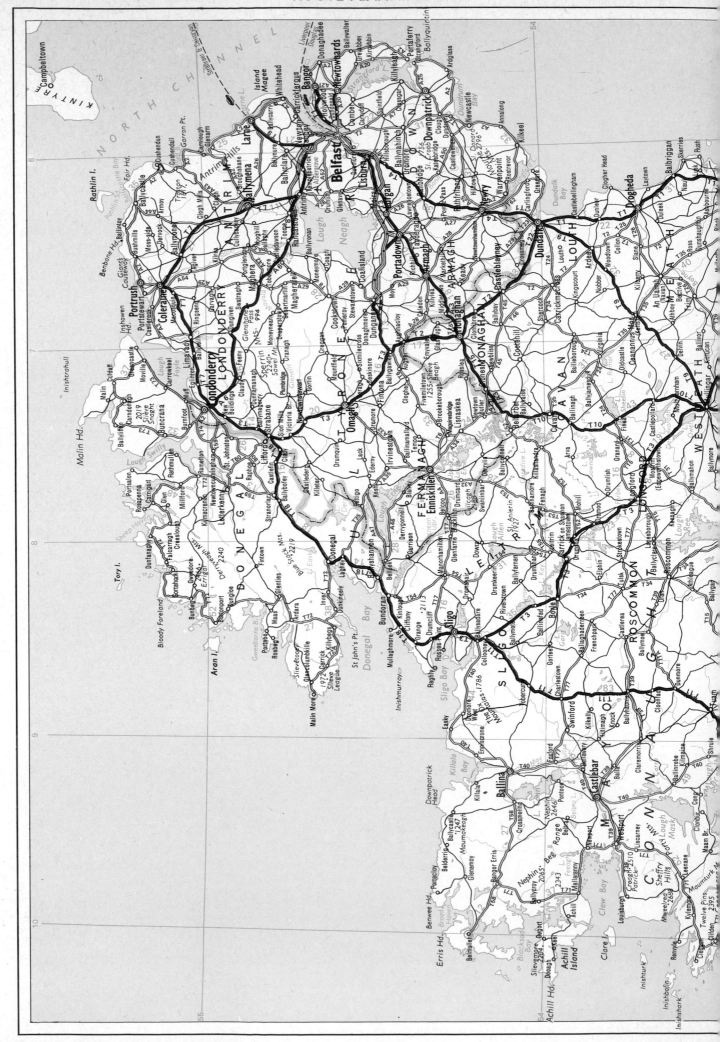

Distances in miles
between circled points 2

1:1 250 000

Heights in feet

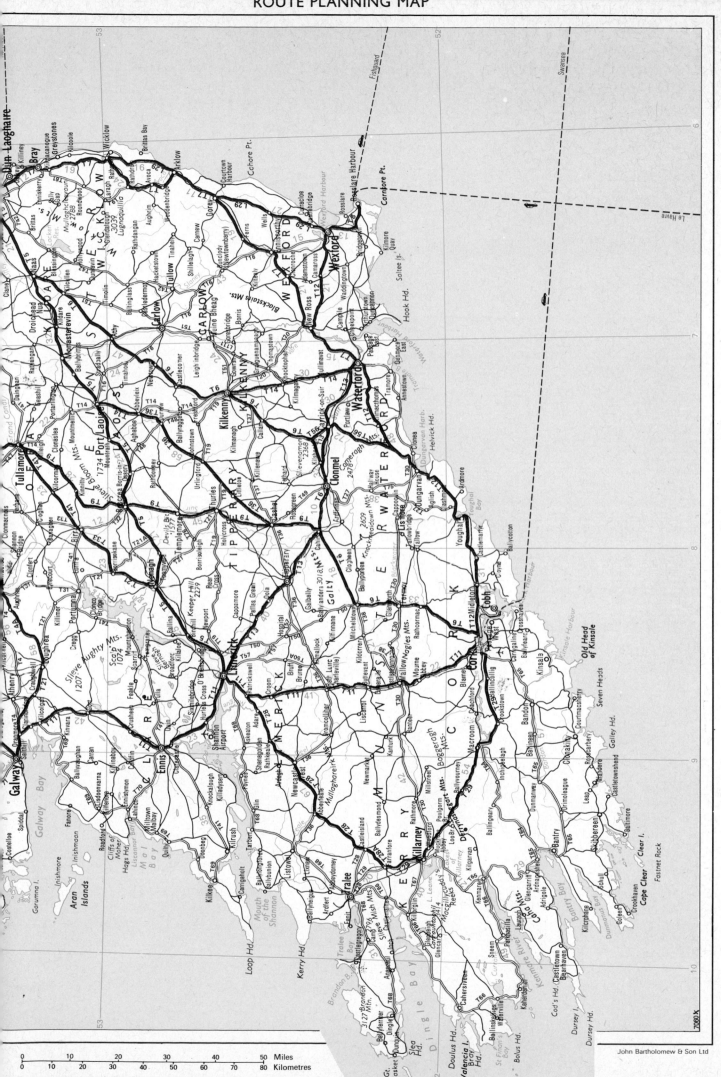